KU-168-495

Disraeli's Reminiscences

EDITED BY
HELEN M. SWARTZ
AND
MARVIN SWARTZ

HAMISH HAMILTON
LONDON

First published in Great Britain 1975
by Hamish Hamilton Ltd
90 Great Russell Street London WC1B 3PT

Copyright © 1975 by Helen M. Swartz
and Marvin Swartz

SBN 241 89288 0

B DIS / B211894

WESTERN EDUCATION

LIBRARY BOARD

Printed in Great Britain by Western Printing Services Ltd, Bristol

CONTENTS

ILLUSTRATIONS

Illustrations 2, 3, 4a, 5a, 5b, 6a, 7b are reproduced by kind permission of the National Trust, Hughenden Manor; 4b and 8 by kind permission of the Victoria and Albert Museum; and 7a by kind permission of the Trustees of the British Museum.

ACKNOWLEDGEMENTS

We are indebted to the National Trust for permission to publish material from the Hughenden Papers. We are especially grateful to the officers and staff of the south-east area office of the National Trust at Hughenden Manor. They, and in particular Barbara Tempest and Barbara North, did their utmost to accommodate us in our research, often at short notice and under difficult circumstances.

A Faculty Growth Grant from the Research Council of the University of Massachusetts at Amherst eased the financial burdens of our work. We thank the librarians at the University, and at Smith College, for their assistance. George Kirk and Hugh Bell were colleagues willing to be importuned by questions, and able to answer them. Our good friend Paul Kennedy was even more helpful than witty.

Finally, the kind hospitality of Margaret and Frank Wise is deeply appreciated. Their patience and understanding have always been greater than the bonds of blood and marriage entitled the editors to expect.

H.M.S.
M.S.

INTRODUCTION

When Benjamin Disraeli wrote these *Reminiscences* in the first half of the 1860's, he could look back upon four decades of striving for literary and political success and social acceptance. He had been a ten-year-old schoolboy in 1815 when the Duke of Wellington defeated Napoleon I at Waterloo. Only with difficulty in the years that followed was the young Disraeli, whose family background was Jewish and middle-class, able to make his way into the aristocratic society that paid homage to the Great Duke. Yet when Wellington died in 1852, the leader of the House of Commons and Chancellor of the Exchequer who eulogized him was Disraeli, for whom greater triumphs were yet to come.

Although personal endeavour and good luck contributed to Disraeli's achievements as a novelist and politician, his family provided him with advantages as well as handicaps. His grandfather was a prosperous businessman whose fortune allowed Disraeli's father, Isaac, to devote himself to literary and scholarly pursuits. In 1791, when he was twenty-five, Isaac D'Israeli published the first volume of the *Curiosities of Literature*, a collection of anecdotes and observations. Further volumes and studies on similar themes appeared at intervals throughout his long life. His works were well known, winning the approval of Byron, Southey, Sir Walter Scott, and Samuel Rogers. The historian Sharon Turner, a close friend, persuaded him to have his children baptized. Isaac introduced his eldest son, Benjamin, born in December 1804, to another friend, the publisher John Murray. He also made arrangements for the boy to be articled to a firm of solicitors.

Benjamin Disraeli, however, abandoned his prospects of entering the legal profession, which seemed to require of its members a sobriety hardly in keeping with the flamboyance of his temperament and dress. During 1825 he speculated in Spanish American mining shares and acted as an assistant to Murray. In the autumn he made two journeys to Scotland as the publisher's emissary to secure the services of J. G. Lockhart, son-in-law of Scott, for a proposed daily newspaper, later named the *Representative*. By the end of the year, having lost a considerable sum of money on the stock exchange, Disraeli withdrew from the newspaper enterprise, which collapsed some months later. Having failed at the age of twenty-one in his first attempts at business and journalism, he was in debt and needed a new source of income and a fresh opportunity to make his name.

In a feverish burst of writing, he completed a novel. Appearing anonymously in April 1826, *Vivian Grey* was a supposed insider's view of high society and a thinly-veiled account of the affair of the *Representative*, at which Murray and his associates took umbrage. The novel immediately attracted attention, but critics were cautious in appraising it until they had discovered the identity of the author. Then, Disraeli, as an impudent youth who had dared to mock a society he hardly knew, had to endure the irate reactions of those who felt themselves duped by his ingenuity or betrayed by his sarcasm. Although he added three volumes to *Vivian Grey* the next year, he suffered a breakdown in health. After recovering gradually at his family's new home, Bradenham Manor, in Buckinghamshire, he was able, in 1830–31, to make a romantic tour of the Mediterranean and the Near East, financed by the advance on *The Young Duke* (1831).

This novel, though little better informed than the first, was less sardonic about that society by which its author desired to be accepted. While writing it Disraeli was forming a firm friendship with, and receiving the advice of, Edward Lytton Bulwer, a novelist and dandy for whose *Pelham* (1828) *Vivian Grey* had furnished inspiration. Bulwer introduced his friend to the London salons of the 1830's that welcomed aspiring dandies, writers, and politicians. Disraeli then frequented the houses of such hostesses as Lady Cork, Lady Jersey, and Lady Blessington (who lived with her son-in-law and presumed lover, Count Alfred D'Orsay). These social contacts stimulated Disraeli's interest in politics and provided colourful material for his novels, including *Henrietta Temple* (1836), drawn in part from a passionate affair with Henrietta Sykes. Although he found the excesses of the early novels an embarrassment as he grew older—later in the *Reminiscences* barely mentioning them—he recollected his social adventures more fondly.

His major concern in the early 1830's, however, was to secure a parliamentary seat. At this time the aristocratic factions of Tories and Whigs were beginning their transformation, as yet ill-defined, into the Conservative and Liberal parties, respectively. Within a year of the passing of the reform bill of 1832, Disraeli had been prepared to stand for parliament four times, on each occasion adapting his politics to constituency and circumstance. He was not returned then, nor in an attempt, at Wycombe, in January 1835. After these failures as an independent radical, though with Tory leanings, he threw in his lot with the Conservative party.

By the mid-1830's Disraeli had some influential Tory patrons, among them Lord Lyndhurst, who probably shared with him the favours of Henrietta Sykes. In April 1835 he was the official Conservative candidate in a by-election at Taunton, which he failed to win, but one observer described him as 'the most intellectual-looking exquisite I had ever seen'.[1] The report of some of his remarks greatly angered the Irish radical Daniel O'Connell and nearly led to a duel. Later that same year Disraeli published, in the form of an open letter to Lyndhurst, a 'Vindication of the English Constitution'. Here he expressed the views which shaped his political thought: as opposed to the selfish and oligarchical Whigs, the Tories were the true majority party and the guardians of English institutions, especially landed property. Supported by Lords Strangford and Chandos, Disraeli was elected in 1836 to the Carlton Club, bastion of Conservative politics.

His first political success was, fittingly, linked to the beginning of the reign of the sovereign whose favour was later to grace the end of his career. The accession of Victoria to the throne followed the death of King William IV in June 1837; so too did a general election. The Carlton Club nominated Disraeli to stand for one of the two seats at Maidstone, and at last, in July, he was elected to parliament. The other seat was held by Wyndham Lewis, who

---

[1] W. F. Monypenny, *The Life of Benjamin Disraeli*, vol. 1 (London, 1910), p. 282.

died within a year. Disraeli, perhaps for affection as well as money, married his widow, Mary Anne, in August 1839.

The slowness of his advancement in the House of Commons irritated Disraeli. He had made his maiden speech in December 1837. It was inauspicious, though he accurately concluded that 'he would sit down now, but the time would come when they would hear him'. In the election of 1841 he was returned for Shrewsbury, but not surprisingly, Sir Robert Peel passed him over when forming his Tory government at the end of the summer. Disraeli was still a new man, without those family connections which have always played so important a part in British politics. Talented, restless, and seething with ambition, he felt aggrieved, perhaps as much at the lack of recognition as at the want of employment.

Probably for this reason he gave much attention in the *Reminiscences* to his visits to France in the first half of the 1840's. There, the revolution of July 1830 had replaced the Bourbon king with the cadet, or Orleanist, branch of the royal family in the person of Louis Philippe. Count Louis Molé, Adolphe Thiers, and especially François Guizot were the important ministers of his regime, which promoted a speculative economic development highly favourable to the enrichment of the upper middle class. Many Englishmen found the social atmosphere in Paris congenial and the French Court less obsessed with protocol than the English. Disraeli and Mary Anne spent the winter of 1842–43 at the Hôtel de l'Europe in the Rue de Rivoli and returned there in December 1845. Little more than two years later Louis Philippe lost his crown as he had won it—on the barricades; he took refuge in England, at Claremont, near Esher, where Disraeli visited him. In retrospect Disraeli attributed a political importance to his activities in Paris which was hardly justifiable, whatever inspiration they provided for his romantic imagination.

The chief beneficiary of the revolution of 1848 in France was another of Disraeli's acquaintances, Prince Louis Napoleon Bonaparte, nephew of Napoleon I. Disraeli had known him in the 1830's as one of the members of the social set gathered round Blessington and D'Orsay at Gore House, Kensington. In those years Louis Napoleon was as inept at making coups d'état as at rowing on the Thames. An abortive coup in 1836 resulted in his banishment from France. A ludicrous landing at Boulogne in

August 1840 led to his arrest and imprisonment. Escaping from the fortress of Ham after more than half a decade, he continued to dream of sitting on the throne of France, as he told Disraeli at a breakfast gathering in June 1846.

At this time Disraeli's hopes for success in politics must have seemed almost as forlorn as Louis Napoleon's, but he too was determined to act. Because he believed that Peel blocked his path to advancement in the Conservative party, Disraeli was prepared, in a political sense, to try to knock down his nominal leader and climb over him. The first instrument he used against Peel was a small ginger group that produced more irritation than effect. 'Young England' consisted of George Smythe (eldest son of the sixth Lord Strangford), Lord John Manners (second son of the fifth Duke of Rutland), and Alexander Baillie Cochrane, all youthful M.P.s educated at Cambridge and more or less under Disraeli's guidance in the House of Commons. It pursued the chimera of romantic Toryism, emphasizing the importance of the landed aristocracy, reluctant to share power and responsibility with the new rich of the industrial age. As throughout his life, Disraeli formed strong bonds of friendship with other men, often in relationships which had many of the attributes of homosexuality.

Young England was active in parliament from 1843 to 1845. It drew varying degrees of support from other Conservative members, including Henry Baillie, Henry Hope (though not his brother Beresford), and Richard Monckton Milnes (son of Pemberton). Disagreement over Peel's proposal for a permanent subsidy for the Catholic seminary at Maynooth in 1845 marked the end of the group's cohesion. Although Disraeli profited little politically from this venture, he gained through it a social entrée into some aristocratic houses. The major significance of Young England for him, however, was literary. Its members and its aspirations helped to inspire his trilogy of the mid-1840's, as well as many of the stories to be found in the *Reminiscences*. In *Coningsby* (1844), *Sybil* (1845), and *Tancred* (1847) he combined his talent for satirical observation with an attempt to examine problems of contemporary political, social, and religious life. He was able by this time, unlike in his earliest novels, to describe members of the aristocracy from personal acquaintance. Although the trilogy provoked widespread discussion and was financially rewarding,

Disraeli was not to publish another novel for more than two decades, as politics had become his consuming interest.

Disraeli continued his battle against Peel with the Protectionist party, composed of those Tories who opposed the Prime Minister's decision to repeal the corn laws. If Young England be likened to a rapier, the protectionist faction was an axe; and with it Disraeli felled Peel. The country gentlemen who supported the cause of protection in 1846 recognized Disraeli's parliamentary abilities, but they were averse to being under his direction. They looked upon him as someone from outside their social sphere, and a Jew. The man who became their leader was Lord George Bentinck, second son of the fourth Duke of Portland. Although he had been private secretary to his uncle by marriage, George Canning (Foreign Secretary and Prime Minister in the 1820's), and an M.P. for nearly two decades, Lord George was best known as a man of the turf.

By serving as Bentinck's second-in-command in the House of Commons, Disraeli assumed a certain acceptability amongst the landed gentry, who, far more than the Peelites or Whigs, needed the political talents he could offer. Bentinck complemented Disraeli without being a rival, for he lacked precisely the political suppleness and oratorical ability which characterized his lieutenant. Although the repeal of the corn laws passed the House in May 1846, Disraeli and Bentinck contributed to turning out Peel on an Irish coercion bill the next month. The Conservatives paid dearly for Peel's obstinacy and Disraeli's ambition: they were not to form a majority government again for a generation—and then with Disraeli at their head.

During the five years after Peel's overthrow, Disraeli won recognition as Protectionist leader in the House of Commons. He became a county member in the general election of 1847, exchanging his borough seat of Shrewsbury for one of the three for Buckinghamshire. The next year he acquired, with the help of a loan from the Bentincks, Hughenden Manor, a modest country estate a mile north of High Wycombe, and thus became, so far as money might permit, a landed gentleman. Before he and Mary Anne moved to their new house, Lord George Bentinck died suddenly at the age of forty-six. Although Disraeli eulogized his friend in *Lord George Bentinck: A Political Biography* (1851), he remarked, according to a cousin of the dead man, that, as Lord

George 'could not lead an Opposition, still less would he have
been able to lead a Government'.[1] For Bentinck had quit as
leader of the Protectionists in the Commons at the beginning of
the session of 1848, after alienating many of his bigoted followers
by favouring, as did Disraeli, a bill to remove the political
disabilities imposed upon Jews. He had, in any case, been disgusted by his inability to control the Protectionist whips, William
Beresford and Charles Newdegate; they took their orders from
Lord Stanley, who sat in the House of Lords and was the acknowledged leader of the party.

After Bentinck's resignation and death, Disraeli was, even more
obviously than before, the one really capable parliamentarian
among the Protectionists in the lower house. He was, however,
less acceptable than Bentinck to the opponents of the 'Jew bill'.
Stanley offered the leadership first to Lord Granby, who took it
and failed miserably within a few weeks, and then to John
Herries, who at three score years and ten had experience enough
to refuse. Finally, in 1849, Stanley proffered the post to Disraeli:
but in a triumvirate with the other two candidates. Well might he
appear a Napoleon in that company! Yet three years passed before
the *primus* could officially rid himself of his *pares*, despite his
subsequent claims of having been leader from 1849 or 1850.

During that time the Conservative party in the House of
Commons remained split. Disraeli headed the Protectionists and
Peel his own followers. Both men sat on the front opposition
bench, separated by the greater or lesser girth of the body or
bodies between them. Disraeli hesitated to bring down the
government that Lord John Russell had formed in July 1846,
because the alternative might have been a ministry dominated by
the Peelites, who possessed in the persons of Sir James Graham,
William Ewart Gladstone, and others, much more talent than did
the Protectionists. Gladstone, not Disraeli, led the unsuccessful
onslaught against Lord Palmerston, the Foreign Secretary, in the
Don Pacifico debate. On the day following the division, 29 June
1850, Peel was thrown from his horse.

Disraeli and other Protectionists, including Lord Londonderry,
paid careful heed to this occurrence; for Sir Robert's death, which

[1] C. C. F. Greville, *A Journal of the Reigns of King George IV. King William
IV. and Queen Victoria*, Henry Reeve, ed., vol. 6 (London, new edn., 1903),
p. 426.

came less than four days later, seemed to offer the possibility of a Conservative reconciliation. Perhaps for this reason Disraeli tried to pretend that there had been no personal rancour between himself and Peel. The latter's followers were unwilling, however, to join forces with the politician who had savagely attacked their fallen leader. Disraeli, too, whatever his arguments afterwards, must have been reluctant to reunite the two elements of the Tory party if to do so would deprive him of the leadership for long. Yet without Peelite cooperation in the House of Commons, the Protectionists were too weak to form a government when Lord John Russell resigned at the opening of the session in 1851. Despite his best efforts, Stanley had to admit the impossibility of the task when, in a meeting on 27 February, he failed to construct a cabinet. The Queen recalled Russell, but his unstable position seemed likely to offer Stanley and Disraeli another chance in the near future.

To take advantage of it, Disraeli believed that the Protectionists would have to abandon the cause which had given them their name. Although the cry of protection was unpopular in the country and alienated the Peelites, it still had supporters who wielded strong influence within and upon the Conservative party. They included the Protectionist Society directed by George F. Young and Stanley's whip, Beresford, who had his master's ear. Disraeli was in part fighting these forces when he put forward his own view of protectionist history in *Lord George Bentinck*; and the recognition of him as sole leader of the party in the House of Commons at the beginning of 1852 was a measure of his progress. By this time Disraeli's political expediency was winning out over the desire for consistency of Lord Derby (Stanley having become the fourteenth Earl in June 1851), although initially his success was more real than apparent.

On 20 February 1852 Disraeli supported Palmerston, who had been dismissed from the cabinet two months earlier, in defeating Russell's government. This time Derby did not hesitate. He agreed to form a ministry, applying not to the Peelites but to Palmerston, under whom Disraeli consented to serve in the Commons. Palmerston refused, Derby's equivocal attitude towards protection proving a sticking point. Disraeli became Chancellor of the Exchequer, holding office for the first time; and Derby managed to fill the remainder of the cabinet positions, though not without some difficulty. So little known were most members of the new government that the Duke of Wellington, now old and deaf, repeatedly exclaimed on being told their names, 'Who? Who?', thereby bestowing a title on the ministry. Three months after the long-lived Duke died in September 1852, the short-lived government expired, having fallen on Disraeli's budget, which Gladstone attacked with telling effect. In his brief tenure of office, however, Disraeli had been able to shunt aside the issue of protection, and he had become a well-known political figure.

During the years that followed he solidified his hold on the Conservative leadership in the House of Commons and strengthened his prominent position in the country. He appointed his own whip, Sir William Joliffe, in place of W. Forbes Mackenzie, who, like Beresford, was tainted with charges of bribery. Disraeli's solicitor, Philip Rose, managed the party organization outside parliament. In May 1853 Disraeli launched a weekly journal, the *Press*, to advertise progressive toryism and to assail the coalition of Whigs and Peelites under Lord Aberdeen which had replaced the Derby government. Disraeli himself contributed articles to the *Press*, as did his friends Bulwer-Lytton and George Smythe. In January 1855 the Crimean war, rather than their writings, brought down Aberdeen.

Once more, Derby had an opportunity, and Disraeli urged him to seize it. The Conservative leader had become more reconciled than formerly to his ambitious lieutenant. He had suspended translating the *Iliad* long enough to entertain Disraeli at Knowsley for the first time in December 1853, though his visitor was not favourably impressed by the house or the social style of his host. Derby, as one of Disraeli's followers observed of the gout-ridden peer, was 'devoted to whist, billiards, racing, betting';[1] he remained a lethargic politician. He declined to take office, and instead Palmerston became Prime Minister in February 1855. Disraeli's criticism of Derby's decision and of Palmerston's war policy, vigorously expressed in the *Press*, helped to keep his relations with many Conservatives cool for the next few years.

He was happy, therefore, to escape to Paris during the winter of 1856–57. There he renewed his acquaintance with Louis

[1] W. F. Monypenny and G. E. Buckle, *The Life of Benjamin Disraeli*, vol. 4 (London, 1916), p. 59.

Napoleon, who, after serving as President of the Republic resulting from the revolution of 1848, had finally achieved his great object: the throne of France. As Napoleon III he greeted Disraeli, who found the Parisian companions of his earlier days as a dandy sadly aged. If he expected to strengthen his domestic political position by hobnobbing with the Emperor, he must have been disappointed. Napoleon III held Disraeli's political abilities in low esteem and judged that the Tories were incapable of over-throwing Palmerston.

So they were, for another year. Then, in February 1858, Palmerston suffered a defeat in parliament and resigned. Derby could not decline office again. He fashioned a stronger cabinet than that of 1852; but the state of the party, still in a minority in the House of Commons, was worse than before. A stumbling block for the Derby government was foreign policy, and specific-ally the Italian question. Count Camillo Cavour was determined to achieve the liberation of Italy from Austrian domination and its unification under the conservative aegis of the Kingdom of Piedmont-Sardinia, of which he was the leading minister. To do so, he forged a secret agreement with Napoleon III in the summer of 1858. The British Court and the Conservatives tended to take the side of Austria, the Liberals and Palmerston that of Italy. The Conservative Foreign Secretary, Lord Malmesbury, tried to prevent a conflict, ultimately sending his ambassador at Paris, Lord Cowley, on a special mission to Vienna. To no avail: war between Austria and the Franco-Italian allies broke out in the spring of 1859.

Meanwhile, the Conservative government was in difficulty. Its failure to carry a reform bill led to a dissolution in April 1859. The ensuing election added to the numbers of Disraeli's followers in the House of Commons, but not sufficiently to secure them an independent majority. Disraeli complicated matters by failing, despite earlier promises, to lay before parliament a blue book of Malmesbury's despatches on the Italian situation; hence his retrospective irritation in the *Reminiscences* with all concerned. An adverse vote on a motion of confidence forced Derby's resignation in June. Palmerston came back in and remained Prime Minister for more than six years, until death loosened his grasp on the supreme prize.

Out of office, as well as in, Disraeli was an amateur dabbler in foreign affairs. He tried to divine the fate of nations from his own prejudices and the personality traits of a few foreign leaders. He exaggerated his influence on Napoleon III, as earlier on Louis Philippe. He also overestimated the power of France, as did most of his contemporaries, and underestimated that of Prussia, which, under the guidance of Otto von Bismarck, began in 1864 the series of wars that were to lead to the unification of Germany. He displayed that English bias against the United States which characterized its people, with some exceptions, as brash and its public life as corrupt. Undoubtedly, he admired Palmerston's success in using foreign policy to transcend domestic difficulties. After Pam died in 1865, Disraeli assumed his role as protector of English interests on the stage of foreign affairs, much as, earlier, he had tried on Peel's mantle of progressive conservatism in the drama of domestic politics. Not surprisingly, in the *Reminiscences* the names of Palmerston and Peel recur more frequently than any others, save that of the fourteenth Earl of Derby.

Despite grumblings within the Conservative party after the defeat of 1859, Disraeli's political prominence brought him increasing social acceptance. He was particularly pleased by the attention he received from the royal family. His sober conduct in office dissipated much of the suspicion his earlier life had aroused in the minds of Queen Victoria and Prince Albert; and his genuine devotion to the monarchy overcame Court resentment of his treatment of Peel. His effusive eulogies after the death of the Prince Consort in December 1861 gratified the bereaved widow. She, at Lord Palmerston's suggestion, invited Disraeli and Mary Anne to the wedding of the Prince of Wales in March 1863; and the next month (April 22–23) he stayed overnight at Windsor Castle, enjoying a personal audience with his sovereign in the morning. Astutely, the Queen did not mention the subject of that afternoon's debate in the House of Commons. She had no need to. Disraeli, at least on this occasion more flattered by her than she by him, went up to London and spoke strongly in favour of voting a grant of £50,000 towards a memorial for Albert.

Disraeli led an active social, as well as political, life in the first half of the 1860's, when he was jotting down the *Reminiscences*. His interest in the classics, literature, and rhetoric did not flag; and he maintained his decided, though odd, views on religion. His social intercourse with such old friends as Lord Lyndhurst, Lady

Jersey, the Rothschilds, and the Caringtons continued. He cultivated useful younger men, especially Lord Stanley, Derby's son, who seemed destined to inherit his father's political position along with his title. He found Baron Brunnow, the Russian ambassador to the Court of St James's, and other diplomatists eager to conevrse with the leader of the opposition in the House of Commons. Appointed a trustee of the British Museum in March 1863, Disraeli took his new duties seriously, as befitted a son of Isaac D'Israeli. When Lord Lyndhurst died at the age of ninety-one in October of that year, his protégé had achieved a measure of success which the old man would probably not have deemed possible a quarter of a century before.

Disraeli took pleasure in being what he considered the posses-sion of Hughenden Manor entitled him to be: one of the country gentlemen of England. He was delighted with his modest estate, which provided him with a quiet haven after the political storms of London. Here he occasionally entertained a few friends or neighbours or allowed his grounds to be used for local fetes or county gatherings. The life of the countryside and its denizens was a source of amusement to him. Perhaps most important, he felt that Hughenden gave him some claim to belong to that society of landed aristocrats whose interests he defended in parliament. In the winter of 1862–63, when Mary Anne was having the appearance of Hughenden Manor transformed from eighteenth-century stucco to nineteenth-century brick with a touch of neo-gothic, he was a guest at Hatfield House, home of the Salisburys. During these and the next few years he was a visitor to various aristocratic houses, great and small, Whig and Tory, and set down on paper some of the gossip he heard there, as well as in the House of Commons.

Although Disraeli's reasons for writing the autobiographical notes which make up these *Reminiscences* are unknown, a number of explanations for his doing so are possible. The composition of one of the notes may date from 1860 and slight additions from as late as 1873 (including a few explanatory comments by Dis-raeli's secretary, Montagu Corry); but Disraeli probably wrote most of them between 1862 and 1866, the bulk of them, appar-ently, in 1863 and 1865. Politically, he was treading water during Palmerston's second ministry, trying to avoid being forced under by the hostility of his own followers and the accomplishments of his successor as Chancellor of the Exchequer, Gladstone. His party duties did not absorb as much of his time as at other periods of his career and, indeed, in many respects must have seemed onerous. Writing was a pleasant occupation and necessary diversion under such circumstances, as it had been in the mid-1840's. In the early sixties, however, he had not yet begun another novel; and illness and death took from him the women who had been his steady correspondents, his sister Sarah, Lady Londonderry, and Sarah Brydges Willyams.

He was also aware that his career was of general public interest. At least two writers preparing biographical sketches of him had asked for information in 1860. Disraeli replied courteously to both, though he warned one of them: 'I am not an admirer of contemporary biography, and I dislike to be the subject of it.'[1] To the other, Francis Espinasse, he supplied a short outline of his life.[2] The next year Espinasse informed him that he was considering being his biographer again but 'on a more extensive scale than on the last occasion'.[3] Disraeli may then have decided to set down on paper some personal recollections. He seems to have abandoned his efforts when the death of Lord Palmerston in October 1865 plunged him once more into the whirl of politics.

Disraeli wrote the *Reminiscences* mainly on sheets of blue or blue-grey paper folded in half to make four pages, each $12\frac{1}{2}$ inches long by 8 inches wide. He used in addition some white or blue-grey sheets folded once into pages 8 by $7\frac{1}{2}$ inches. A few single sheets or small white scraps also form part of the original collection. The seventy-seven sections vary in length from one to twenty-three pages. Approximately half of them contain paper with watermarks, bearing mostly the dates 1822, 1854, 1863, and 1865.

The distribution of watermarks, as well as internal evidence in the manuscript sheets, prove that the order of the papers (in Box 26, A/X/A) at Hughenden is not the order in which Disraeli wrote them. The latter is now impossible to determine. We did not feel obliged to retain a format which was, it seems, designed, after Disraeli's death, to aid in constructing a biography of the

---

[1] Disraeli to T. E. Kebbel, 25 Nov. 1860: in T. E. Kebbel, *Lord Beaconsfield and Other Tory Memories* (New York, 1907), p. 27.

[2] See Appendix.

[3] F. Espinasse to Disraeli, 12 June 1861: Hughenden Papers A/X/B/5.

author. We have instead adopted the approach of grouping the
sections, roughly, in the chronological order of their contents,
though with some consideration also to the date of composition,
so far as this could be worked out. We have provided a key (pp.
152–3) that will enable any interested scholar to compare this
published edition with the original manuscript. We have reproduced all the sections in their entirety. In doing so we respected
the integrity of individual sections, despite temptations to dis-
member some of them, because we could not be sure of devising
any better method of putting them together again. They convey
the episodic way in which Disraeli wrote them, as more or less
associated thoughts came into his mind, perhaps in pacing up and
down the terrace at Hughenden.

Probably for this reason the manuscript is replete with problems for the editor. We have not retained spelling mistakes, errors
of usage, or except in a few instances, abbreviations. We have
added a minimum of punctuation, and infrequently subtracted
some mark, in order to avoid complete confusion. When absolutely necessary, we have added words to the text in brackets. As
editors, we considered that these minimal changes were preferable
to the constant distractions that an exact reproduction of the
manuscript would entail. Disraeli's use of 'American' spelling (for
such words as 'honor' and 'favor'), though not always consistent,
has not been altered. The footnotes, with a few exceptions, contain textual variations, usually superscriptions, sometimes put in
at a later date.

Finally, factual errors abound. Disraeli was a politician and
novelist, not an historian. Some critics might call him a liar. He
wrote down these stories not only for their intrinsic interest but
also for the purpose of putting the past into the perspective from
which he wanted it to be viewed. He may have intended them to
form the basis for a biography; and they were indeed heavily
mined by Monypenny and Buckle half a century later. He certainly
used some of the stories found in the *Reminiscences* in *Lothair*
(1870) and *Endymion* (1880), his last two novels. Naturally,
Disraeli made mistakes, unconscious or conscious, in recounting
these tales. Often, too, he was vague about details, as might be
any writer who jots down quickly the outline of a story as it
flows through his mind and onto the page. We have not attempted
to straighten out the kinks in Disraeli's account with an accom-

panying commentary of our own. This the scholar does not need nor the general reader want, certainly not in the fullness that would have been required.

Our desire has been to present Disraeli 'undiluted'.[1] We hope that the reader will be able to discover answers to his questions by referring to this introduction and to the index, which includes identifications as they pertain to this work. He can begin to satisfy any further curiosity about Disraeli and his times by looking at some of the books listed in the short bibliography. The *Reminiscences* are Disraeli's closest approach to non-fictional autobiography, and they contain some of his finest and wittiest writing. May the reader enjoy them.

[1] Cf. below, p. 31.

Disraeli's Reminiscences

I

'UNKNOWN TO FAME'

[1]

When unjustly attacked wanted to write a letter in the newspapers & consulted the Duke of Wellington (1st Duke), his Grace was against it. He said 'Never explain: this is a nine days' wonder; but every explanation is another nine days' wonder.'

The Duke of Wellington's mother, the old Countess of Mornington, was one of the wickedest women that ever lived, a female tyrant of the middle ages, or what we sometimes read of in oriental history—the temper of a daemon heartless & debauched.

When Lord Mornington woke in the morning he rang for his valet & used to say 'Has your lady rung her bell?' 'Yes; my Lord.' 'How is she?' 'Well my lord I hear she is very crump.' 'Oh! then you lock my door, & go away with the key in your pocket.'

The Duke of Wellington's real father was General, the Hon. Gardiner, son of Lord Blessington. When the Duke showed his alleged parents' portraits, he used to say 'Here is Lord Wellesley's father: & here is my mother.'

The Duke when a youth was at the military academy at Angers, & Lord & Lady Mornington being at Paris, & returning to England, arranged to go home by Angers & take Arthur with them. This, to a certain degree, accordingly took place, but when they were on their road, after Angers, Lady Mornington said that Arthur had kicked her shin in the carriage, & ordered him to be put out on the road—& there he was left with what pocket money he might chance to have.

Sometime after this Lady Mornington was at the Opera with Lady   ,* who told this to the Duke, & Lady Mornington said 'Why, I declare, there's my ugly son, Arthur.'

She never at any time in the least recognised the talents or

* Disraeli's blank.

5

position of her children: never said anything to them which intimated that she thought them superior to other men. She always mortified them or tried to.

After Waterloo, or certainly after the peace of Paris, the Duke & Lord Wellesley who had been Viceroy of India & the other three brothers (one an ambassador & another a Minister of State?) all dined with her; I think it must have been at Hampton Court. She was never more detestable. When the brothers were alone, they held a sort of public meeting & passed resolutions.

1st That their mother was as *'crump'* as ever

2nd That they did not care for it half as much as they used to.

[2]

Lady Ebury said that she 'lived for Climate & the affections'. Two good things.

Sir James Macintosh said that 'Of all delusions that existed, Posthumous Fame was the greatest.'

He said this to my father—but it may be a question in what sense it was uttered. He may have meant, it was a delusion so far as people expecting to attain it—for it is the lot of a few—you may number them on your finger—but my father understood it, at the time, as a delusion per se.

Gladstone said he had a good memory, but not for passages. He never could command them. (At the Academy dinner, I sate next to him.)

My grandfather knew Cagliostro: i.e. he was in the habit of meeting him, at Cosway's, a famous person himself in his day. Maria Cosway held a salon, & it was attended much by the mystics, the illuminati & people of that class; & a great many people of fashion also. My grandfather said, that he never could understand the great space which Cagliostro filled in men's thoughts & conversation. He would say this still more now. The French Revolution, & so many vast events & changes, & yet Cagliostro frequently mentioned. He said, that C. was, without exception, the vainest being, that he ever came across. This was the key of his character, of his life, his history. He acquitted him of mean motives in his most ambiguous proceedings. If he obtained money in a queer manner, it was only, that he might lavish it like a prince & often on princely objects. He was so flattered by being supposed to have discovered the philosopher's stone, that he would give a man fifty guineas who told him so, though it was the last fifty guineas he had.

He was a man of restless imagination & almost believed at last in his own singular impostures, which were all about himself. He started in life as the son of a Grand-Master of Malta by the daughter of the Great Sheikh of Arabia—conveyed early to the Desert & brought up there, & then sent to Europe (to Malta first, I believe,) for a complete education. And this was believed! Indeed this part of his history was never exposed. Accepted. What a wonderful age. Not a century ago! But no telegrams, no railroads, scarcely any newspapers.

His person was not distinguished. He was short & dark. But with soft, insinuating manners, & wonderful eyes.

He was in reality a Jew; his name Joseph Balsamo (i.e. son of Solomon) & born in Calabria. Possibly, he may have known a little Hebrew, which might have helped him in the tongue, which he spoke as an Arabian Prince. But in that part of the world, a bastard Arabic (common in Malta & called Smiche, & in Calabria too) is very prevalent.

There was another man, who was of the same class, at Cosway's —Loutherbourgh the artist.

My grandfather came across him suddenly one day, making the Hebrew reverences, & he confessed to him, that he also was a son of Israel.

[3]

When my father published the second part of the *Curiosities of Literature*, & much the finest, in 1822, Palgrave (afterwards Sir Francis) said to him 'I look upon it as the greatest Belles Lettres book this age has produced, but then I consider the age of Belles Lettres to have passed.' My father was of the same opinion as Palgrave, & thought that Science would supersede what is called Literature.

No doubt, in a certain sense, it has in those superior circles which had exhausted Literature, but they did not estimate the new reading classes who would arise, & to whom Literature was as strange & as fascinating as Science.

My father lived more than a quarter of a century after this observation, & published before his death in 1848 more numerous & larger editions of *C. of L.* than during his preceding life. And since his death, the *Curios* & all his merely literary works have been stereotyped, & are sold at every Railway stall of the Kingdom, & are the favorite reading in this kind of the bustling & toiling millions.

[4]

Elmley was always saying 'What did Jesus do before he was thirty? My conviction is, that he must have had an eventful youth, & that he had travelled a great deal.' This travelling of Jesus was a great point with Elmley. He frequently recurred to it. I never could agree with him. It seemed such an original mind; so completely formed in seclusion, & with all its Shakespearian genius, so essentially local. All the illustrations are drawn from inward resources, or from surrounding scenery.

The intellectual expression of Macaulay's countenance was magnificent—never on a nobler forehead, piled up with sagacity & depth. He was a splendid orator; a writer of the first class, both in originality of treatment & power of expression; his learning was very extensive & very various. No man ever had a memory at the same time so prodigious, & so cultivated. He left an ample fortune. He never spent a shilling of what he had made by his pen. Sir Chas Trevelyan, his brother in law, told me this at the Treasury, when I was Chancellor of the Exchequer in 1858. It must have been before Macaulay's death.* Early in life, he was made a Commissioner of Bankrupt, under the old regime; which was then for a young Barrister like a fellowship at College: three or four hundred a year—& he had always, I believe, his Trinity fellowship. Then he was sent in 1834 (I think 1834) by the Whigs

* Uncertain of the date of Macaulay's death, Disraeli wrote 'Query?' above this line.

to India with 10,000£ per annum & he returned with some considerable savings.

I said to Sir Charles, that if it were a fair question, I should like much to know, what was the amount that Macaulay had made by his pen—but to have no delicacy in refusing me the information. On the contrary he said he would tell me with the utmost readiness. The sum was 60,000£ (sixty thousand pounds).

I regret, that I did not enquire whether this was the result of accumulated interest or of absolute payments.

Macaulay had fame at school & at college & from his writings in Knight's Magazine. But what gave him his great start & gave him public fame, was his article in the *Edinburgh Review* on Milton. Which reminds me of a curious circumstance.

When I was quite a youth (1825) I was travelling in Scotland, & my father gave me a letter to Sir Walter Scott. I visited him at Abbotsford. I remember him quite well. A kind, but rather stately, person—with his pile of forehead, sagacious eye, white hair & green shooting coat. He was extremely hospitable; & after dinner, with no lack of claret, the quaighs & whiskey were brought in. I have seen him sitting in his arm chair, in his beautiful library, which was the chief rendezvous of the House, & in which we met in the evening—with half a dozen terriers about him—in his lap, on his shoulders, at his feet. 'These' he said 'to me are Dandie Dinmont's breed.' They were all called Mustard & Pepper, according to their color & their age.

He would read aloud in the evening, or his daughter, an interesting girl, Anne Scott, would sing some ballad on the harp. He liked to tell a story of some Scotch chief, & sometimes of some Scotch lawyer.

I was at Abbotsford again later in the year for a day. The *Edinburgh Review* had just arrived. Mr Lockhart, then about thirty or so but a very experienced literary man, I remember saying 'Well, they may say what they like, but no man can write like Jeffrey on poetry. The article on Milton in the new number is the finest thing we have had for years.'

As I came down to dinner, Sir Walter was walking up & down the hall with a very big, stout, florid man, apparently in earnest conversation. I was introduced to him before dinner as Mr Constable, the famous publisher of the *Edinburgh Review* & the Waverley novels, the authorship of them not then acknowledged, at least, not formally. It struck me, that I had never met before such an ostentatious man, or one whose conversation was so braggart. One would think that he had written the Waverley novels himself, & certainly that Abbotsford belonged to him. However he seemed to worship Scott, & to express his adoration. His carriage was announced, while he was at dinner, & he was obliged to go, as he had to return to Edinburgh to transact some business & then go up to London by the morrow's mail, by which also I was to return.

So we met again, & I sate opposite him. He put a rich velvet cap with a broad gold band on his head, & looked like a great heraldic Lion crowned. We had two fellow passengers, I am sure, but I don't recollect anything about them. But I never shall forget Constable's conversation. It was only about Abbotsford & the Waverley novels. He informed me that he intended to build a new wing to Abbotsford next year & you would have supposed from what he said that Sir Walter had only commenced developing a new Eldorado. I never in my life met such a braggart, or a man so full of self-importance. Something had gone wrong in the journey; the guard or the coachman had displeased. He went into an ecstasy of pompous passion. 'Do you know Who I am, man? I am Archibald Constable'—&c &c &c. This man was on the point of a most fatal & shattering bankruptcy; had gone up to town with some desperate resolve; & in less than a week the crash came.

When he had exhausted Abbotsford & the Waverley novels, he began bragging about the *Edinburgh Review*—& dilated much on an article on Milton. I, like a youth, repeating at second-hand, ventured to observe, that no one wrote on Poetry like Jeffrey. I copied this from Lockhart, but I flatter myself, that if I had read the article, I should not have made the observation; for it always afterwards gave me a very low opinion of Lockhart's literary discrimination. No man with a good nose could have [supposed] for an instant that Jeffrey had written the article in question.

Constable informed me, that it was not by Jeffrey, but that it was a secret—but so little was his power of reserve & reticence, or so great the excitement under which he then laboured, that before long I had no difficulty in worming out from him, that it was by a young lawyer of the name of Macaulay, from whom he expected great things. Therefore I arrived in London with a sort of literary secret.

[5]

Croker never got free of his brogue. Dining once, at my father's, the conversation falling on the authorship of Junius, Croker said 'One thing is quite clear; Junius was a parson—'

'Good God!' said my father involuntarily interrupting him, 'this is the first time that I ever heard, that Junius was a clergyman.'

'Person, person' said Croker.

'Don't look at that' said the Duke of Devonshire to Lady Jersey at Chatsworth, as he was shewing her some portraits in the Gallery. 'She brought us a great deal of money, but she brought us our hideousness. The Cavendishes were a very handsome family till that alliance. And what's worse' he continued 'it is not us only, but she has transmitted her hideousness to every family that has allied itself with us. It's the origin of the Howard face, & others.' His Grace was speaking of a portrait of a Duchess of Devonshire —the heiress of a Mr., or a Sir George, Hodgkinson of Middlesex, & who had so fatally stamped her image on some of our patrician races.

[6]

Lord Willoughby de Eresby, a great aristocrat, with remarkable simplicity of manners, used in a humorous, demure, way, to quiz the ultra-educational movement, especially among the London Gamins. 'We are educating them' he would say '& they are far beyond us. They shut one up in a moment. I was walking with Flahault the other day, & there was a knot of boys, they filled the pavement; one could not pass. I laid my hand on the shoulder of an urchin, & asked in the gentlest manner permission to pass. Upon which he said 'Who gave you leave to go out alone?' Willoughby & Comte Flahault were the two most courteous men in London, of the high old school of grand manners. Fancy them bowing to these gamins!

Then Lady Willoughby had a school in London in which she took a great interest & to which she never could induce Lord

Willoughby to go. At last one day she prevailed upon him. He
was to meet her there & went, I think, with William Rose. Being
a man who was always behind his time, he only arrived when the
school was breaking up. There was a crowd of urchins, & one
boy, about twelve caught his eye. He rushed like the others out
of the school, & then took a short pipe out of his pocket, began
filling it with tobacco, & striking a light. 'My dear child' said
Lord Willoughby advancing to him in horror. 'Do you know,
that if you go on with this dreadful practice, you will never reach
twenty one years of age?'

'And a damned good thing, if I don't' said the urchin.

So much for Lady Willoughby's London School.

1830

Just at the commencement of this Spring if Spring it could be
called, early in March, in my way to Falmouth, to embark for
Gibraltar, I made the acquaintance of Lytton Bulwer, & dined
with him at his house in Hertford Street. He was just married, or
about just married—a year or two. We were both of us then quite
youths; about four & twenty. I met three men at dinner of much
the same standing; all full of energy & ambition, & all unknown
to fame. Bulwer & I had, at least, written something; I 'Vivian
Grey', & he two or three years afterwards 'Pelham'. The other
three were Henry Bulwer, Charles Villiers, & Alexander Cockburn. Writing this, nearly 5 & 30 [years] afterwards, it is curious
to mark what has been the result of the careers of these five young
men.

I have been twice Leader of the House of Commons. Edward
Bulwer has been Secretary of State. Henry Bulwer is at this
moment H.M. Ambassador at Constantinople. Charles Villiers is
at this moment a Cabinet Minister. & Alexander Cockburn is Lord
Chief Justice of England.

[7]

Rogers of Lord Grey, *1832* 'Singular man! Without wit, taste, or
eloquence, & yet when he speaks, the whole sex at his feet!'

He spoke with his right hand in his breast, & his right leg
advanced & foot turned out.

Evidently a man taught to speak, & rolling his body up & down.

'Great sprawling legs.'

Certainly a great power of language—but then you remembered nothing he ever said.

Lady Jersey

[8]

In the early Reform years, probably when William 4th had lost the affections of the Radicals, the King was very much attacked in the House of Commons on some matter by Hume & Roebuck. His Majesty said to Lord John Russell 'The Sovereign of England is not going to be bullied by a retired East India Surgeon, & a Canadian Miniature painter.'

Lord John Russell told me this himself. I was not aware before of Roebuck's origin. It has been kept very close.

Old Lord Londonderry (the Minister's brother) told me that there used to be great dissensions between his parents about cutting down trees. His mother was very opposed to this necessary & salutary process—when judiciously carried on. After her death, some verses were found in her papers, addressed to her husband, & they began

'Avaunt! Arboricide!'

[9]

How little we know ourselves. When Lord Wellesley lost his post as Lord Lieutenant of Ireland & heard that his successor was the Marquess of Anglesey, he exclaimed 'What an appointment! A cockscomb! A Spendthrift! An Adulterer!'

D'Orsay, who was a very clever artist, painted Lord Wellesley, who was his near neighbour at Kensington Gore, & very successfully. Afterwards the Duke of Wellington sate to him. The Duke was fascinated by D'Orsay, & delighted in his own portrait. It has been engraved. The Duke said 'D'Orsay is the only painter

who ever made me look like a gentleman.' Calling on D'Orsay
one day in his studio, the Duke's portrait being on an easel, &
that of the Marquess Wellesley, his brother, framed & suspended,
D'Orsay said, looking from the easel to the framed picture 'Cock
pheasant & Hen pheasant!'

After D'Orsay's death, they tried to make out that his art was an
imposture, & that it was all done by artists in his pay. No doubt
he employed men, who worked under him, & in some points
more technical than he was—but the quick perception & the
catching of character were all his own, & the general conception
of the work. In this he was very remarkable. The day after Lord
George Bentinck's death he commenced a small bust of him from
memory. It is a speaking likeness—all the character of the man as
he sate in the House of Commons. I saw D'Orsay at work upon
this: its execution was very rapid. No mechanical artist did, or
could, help him in this affair. They didn't know the man, & there
was not a portrait, with the exception of a very early & very bad
one by a Lynn artist, statue, or bust of George Bentinck in
existence. The statue by Campbell in Cavendish Square was made
up. I lent him D'Orsay's bust, which is at Hughenden, & he had
an engraving from the bad picture (for, in default of a better, we
had that engraved for his friends. It has not the slightest resemblance to him) & all George Bentinck's aunts & sisters went &
criticised the work as it proceeded. It is a sad affair. Campbell
however could hardly be blamed. He executed afterwards a bust
of Bentinck in marble, in which he was greatly guided by my
wife. I had wished to have purchased this, but he had offered it
to the Trustees of the National Gallery—of which I was one & I
of course withdrew from competition under such circumstances.
So it was purchased, with my approval, for the nation.

II

ORLEANIST AND BONAPARTIST

[10]

General Baudrand, Governor of the Comte de Paris, & entirely devoted to the House of Orleans—a man who had risen from the ranks, I believe, but a natural nobleman—a man of the highest moral tone as well as social breeding, doing every justice to the King to whom he was attached, often concluded his confidential observations by saying 'What the King wants is *dignity*'—'C'est que le Roi manque—c'est la dignité.'

Baudrand without stiffness, for he was genial, had as great a share of dignity as I ever met.

King Louis Philippe sent Baudrand on his accession to the Duke of Wellington to explain everything, & obtain an immediate recognition.

Baudrand's account of his interview with the Duke [was] very interesting. Wellington was not so grieved about the '3 glorious days' as some suppose. The elder branch, in their anxiety to become popular, were going very wrong, & were about to attack the Rhine. The Duke accepted the election of the House of Orleans as a pledge for constitutional & moderate government.

Baudrand was exactly the envoy the Duke would appreciate—a distinguished soldier, with a simplicity like his own.

[11]

Bulwer, who then lived at Craven Cottage, gave a breakfast party there. We arrived late, & all the guests had gone up the Thames in a steamer. Walking on the Terrace, quite alone, two gentlemen who had arrived still later came up to us. These were Prince Louis Napoleon & Persigny (after Ham). My wife explained to

17

the Prince why the assembly was so scant. Upon which the Prince
said 'We will get a boat, & I will row you down to meet them.'

There was a boat & boatman lingering about, whom we hailed
from the Terrace. The Prince took the oars, & for a little time
we went on very well. At last to escape the swell of a steamer, that
was approaching the Prince contrived to row into a mud bank
in the middle of the river—& there we stuck. Nothing could get
us off. I was amused by the manner in which my wife, who was
alarmed, especially, & not without cause, from the fear of other
steamboats which caused a great swell on the water, rated the
Prince 'You should not undertake things, which you cannot
accomplish. You are always, Sir, too adventurous' &c &c &c. I
remained silent. At length, the boatman, who had come to the
rescue, got us off, & we arrived again at Craven Cottage, just as
Bulwer's company appeared in the distance. Nothing could be
more goodnatured than the Prince—& I could not have borne the
scolding better myself. We often used to smile over this adventure
—& many years after, (I think 1856) my wife sate next to the
Emperor at dinner at the Tuileries, & as he was chatty, & often
adverted to the past, she ventured to remind His Majesty of the
story, which he said he quite remembered. The Empress, who
overheard them, said 'Just like him'.

Louis Napoleon was a very goodnatured man; & his impulses
were generally right. The first Emperor was not so. He was
naturally tyrannical & vindictive. There was no similarity in their
organisation. One was Corsican: it was said the other was
Barbarian—but anyrate on his mother's side, he was French. That
mixture had mitigated a sound, sterner foundation.

Most curious, that after the 1st Napoleon had repudiated
Josephine for the sake of a dynasty, his descendant is not on the
throne of France, while unquestionably the grandson of Josephine
is.

So, it may be said, the great divorce ended in establishing the
dynasty of Josephine.

Old Goldsmith more than once told me, that when he received a
message from the 1st Buonaparte to attend him at the Tuileries it
always gave him a stomachache, & sometimes brought on diar-
rhoea.

[12]

A list of the guests who dined with the Emperor at his residence at Carlton Terrace a few days before the Boulogne expedition. All dead except Persigny.

Nov. 1860

Ogle gave me this list at Spa 1856-or 7—his father then alive & now he is dead—young like many of the others.

> The Emperor
> Persigny
> General Montholon
> Admiral Ussher   (Bellero)
> D'Orsay
> Lord Allen
> Sir G. Wombwell
> Lord Adolphus FitzClarence   *
> Power the actor
> Sir Massey Stanley
> Ogle—afterwards Sir Chaloner Ogle

[13]

When I was in Paris *1842*?, the Court was slowly recovering from the death of the Duke of Orleans. The King, however, was full of confidence in himself & in his dynasty. He dwelt on the resemblance of the position of William 3rd of England & himself. He had this additional advantage: children.

The greatest contrast was afforded between the private lives of the Rothschilds & the Hopes. The prosperity of the Rothschilds was as much owing to the unity of feeling which alike pervaded all branches of that numerous family as on their capital & abilities. They were like an Arabian tribe. The three brothers Hope, however, though the wealth of the whole family of Hope had become concentrated in them, were always at war. There were some famous jewels, which had belonged to their uncle Philip Hope,

* Written down the right margin: 'My My My'.

which were a fruitful subject of litigation. There was a blue
diamond, that all the brothers wanted. They hated each other.
Neither Adrian nor Beresford Hope, went to their brother's
bedside, though he was dying, & long dying, & had a couple of
millions, at least, to bequeath. He left it all to his French mistress
whom he had married a few years before his death.

Henry Hope had good abilities & was not incapable of affection, but suspicion embittered his life. It was his sovereign
malady.

When I entered the House of Commons & for some time afterwards the North of England carried everything before it. Lord
Stanley, & afterwards his son, Sir Robert Peel, Sir James Graham,
Gladstone, Cobden,* Bright, Sir Charles Wood, the Greys, were
all north-country men. Lord John was leader of the House to be
sure, & he was South, but he was alone. When I became leader
of the opposition in 1849, the two leaders were South; Beds &
Bucks;—& then Sidney Herbert began to take a leading place
& Sir George Lewis, & Palmerston commenced to take a greater
part in debate & ultimately became Leader—& the preponderance
of the South seemed not impossible. But Herbert & Lewis soon
died & Lord John went to the Upper House. At present the two
leaders are both South, & the balance is generally more equal.

[14]

I had my first audience with King Louis Philippe at St. Cloud at
the end of the autumn of 1842. The exact time might be known by
this. While I was waiting in the antechamber, one of the King's
aides-de-camp brought me from his Majesty the telegram?†
announcing the triumphant entrance of the English, under
General Pollock, into Cabul.

The audience was long & not formal. It was the only time in
my experience in which the King did not engross the conversation, & few foreigners have enjoyed so great an intimacy with
that sovereign as myself. I have been in the habit of remaining
after the evening receptions at the Tuileries, & sitting with him
in his Cabinet until a very late hour, he himself dismissing me by

---

* '? no' above Cobden's name, quite rightly.

† '(despatch)' written above.

a private way, as all the Royal Household had retired. In these conversations, or rather communications, he seemed to conceal from me nothing. Sometimes, he would speak only of his early life; his strange adventures, escapes, hardships, & necessities. The last time I was alone with him in 1846 (Jany.) he had indulged in this view, & in reply to an observation which I had made I remember well his saying 'Ah! Mr Disraeli, mine has been a life of great vicissitude!'

He would always speak English with me. He had a complete command of our language; even of its slang (*argot*). Perhaps it might be said, that his English was a little American.

In 1842 the King was entirely master—his own chief Minister in fact. He was fond of affairs, & jealous of the interference or aspirations of his sons. The Duke of Orleans was just dead. The King had a conviction that he thoroughly understood Frenchmen, & knew how to manage them. He despised his people. More than once when I had made a suggestion, he would remark 'Ah! I have to deal with a very different people from you.' And then a peculiar grimace of contempt & dislike. 'The way to manage these people is to give them their head, & then know when to pull them up.'

Guizot's manner had no charm—it was indeed repulsive—not exactly pedantic, but professorial: hard, dogmatic, arrogant. His countenance very fine; a brow of beaming intellect, & a won-drous* eye. His general countenance often reminded me of Roubiliac's bust of Pope.

Thiers looked & chattered like a little Journalist; a monkey, but wonderfully sharp & self complacent & clever.

Affairs were changed in 1846.

Guizot was rooted in power—& had persuaded the King, that he was the Richelieu of a Louis 14. Thiers, who had a considerable following in 1842–3—the remains of his position in 1839 of first Minister, was greatly sunk—had reverted to literature—& was very disaffected. The Hotel Molé had been pulled down & the Comte lived in a new one in the moorish quarter of Faubourg St. Honoré. His chance seemed quite to have vanished.

(See Life of Ld G. Bentinck p. 236–40 for an account of what took place between L.P. & D. in 1845–6).

* 'flashing' written faintly above.

The anticipations of the King as to the effect of Lord Palmerston returning to office, soon realised—estrangement between the two Courts in consequence of the Spanish match. Restless state of Europe—the Minto mission—Reform question at Paris—Meeting of Parliament, 1848, George Smythe (Strangford) brought the last news from Paris. He had been Under Secretary of State with Lord Aberdeen, & had had a conversation with Guizot at his reception. G.S.S. considered affairs at Paris critical, but described Guizot as 'transcendentally bumptious'.

Comte de Jarnac at the Coventry Club on the critical day—a little nervous but most sanguine.

'What do you think?' he said to me.

'I cannot doubt but with such notice & such men all must be prepared.'

He nodded entire assent, & said 'It must be right.'

I did not know then, that he had at that time, though I should think not more than thirty years of age, his appointment as *Ambassador of France* to our Court, I may say, in his pocket. But he bore his bitter disappointment well. Seldom a greater fall. He had to retire to Ireland, having married, & live on a meagre paternal allowance—& occupied himself with writing a novel, instead of living in a palace, with a large revenue, & writing despatches on the fate of the world.

This was at the Coventry Club, where only a season before, the same Comte Jarnac exerted all his influence to secure the black-balling of Louis Napoleon.

The Coventry was a very exclusive club of fine gentlemen, a sort of Boulevard White's. Coventry House, opposite the Green Park—much frequented in the summer time, when a Club in a street was said to be intolerable & where the members indulged in drinking sherry cobbler through quills—an American beverage & fashion. They had the famous Francatelli for their cook, who had been expelled the royal household because he had attempted to assassinate one of his marmitons. But the Coventry was indulgent to the irritability of men of genius.

One of the main elements of the Coventry was the *diplomatic*. Brunnow was one of its chief originators, in consequence of a quarrel with White's, of which he was a member, some Russian Prince not having been admitted. Lord Shelburne, who asked me to belong to it, was also one of the founders.

HUGHENDEN MANOR

'sauntering about my park and . . . in the library'

BENJAMIN DISRAELI

'complete domestic happiness . . . has mainly sustained me in a
career of considerable trial'

MARY ANNE DISRAELI
'my guardian angel'

LOUIS PHILIPPE
'full of confidence in himself
and in his dynasty'

NAPOLEON III
'a very romantic man'

The Club was too exclusive to last long under any circumstances perhaps; but it ultimately was broken up in consequence of a portion of the members playing lansquenet, it having been one of the original conditions that no games of chance should be allowed. These very fashionable clubs cannot flourish without being night clubs—there must be suppers after the Opera, & after everything else—& if young men meet at a Club at night they will play. There was then a great prejudice against play—Crockford's having worn out, & it was resolved that the Coventry should not tolerate it.

The Coventry was, however, for a season, the great resort of distinguished foreigners. The Duke of Parma, who was afterwards assassinated, was an habitué of the Coventry—he was a very droll man, exceedingly amusing & clever—a rattle, a mimic, & gambolled in mind & body. He was a great tumbler & skilful in all sorts of tours de force. Walking with the Queen at Windsor, & I believe the first time, he suddenly tumbled before her Majesty the whole way as she walked. She died with laughter & astonishment. He was less like a tyrant than any person I ever met: full of fun & humor. He enjoyed English & club life, & after he had been restored to his dominions, paid a visit to England, came immediately to the Coventry, & called for some sherry cobbler.

[15]

At Paris in 1842–3 Guizot, Minister, but not supposed to be very strong. His strength increased with the strength of Peel, & Madame Lieven consolidated the alliance between Guizot & Lord Aberdeen. His rivals were Thiers, who had been Minister, & was leader of the Opposition, & Comte Molé, descendant of the Grande Barbe & inheriting not merely his name, but the honors & estates of the family, for Molé had been a minor in the days of the Emigration, remained in France under wise guardians, & preserved the whole of his estates, which during his life time, the Code Napoleon, almost as bad as the emigration, could not diminish. Molé was a grandseigneur of the highest breeding; courtly, finished, dignified if necessary, but easy & simple. Excellent talents, very general information, a complete political culture, & not a mean orator when under pressure. He was supposed to lean to the Russian alliance; though I believe this was only a newspaper theory. I was on terms of great intimacy with him, & he spoke freely to me of his views as regards England.

He was short in stature, like his rivals Guizot & Thiers. His countenance was dark with regular features of the Jewish cast, & he was supposed to inherit his physiognomy from the famous Hebrew heiress, Mademoiselle de Bernard, who married into his family in the year   .* Comte Molé was considered fitful— unequal & uncertain in his efforts. The truth is he labored under a great & very singular disqualification which was little known, but which was really the key to his character & conduct. His functions only moved once in ten days. If you had met him the day on which he had experienced relief, you would have thought him one of the most brilliant men you had encountered: witty, gay, full of playfulness & resource. The same on the second, almost on the third. As time advanced, there was a gradual change. Days still remained, that he was able & effective, though with an exertion; but as the crisis grew nearer, he became more & more incapable of affairs; irritable, obscure, confused, & at length irrisible. There was no person, therefore, of whom you could hear more contrary accounts & characters than of Comte Molé.

He lived in the Hotel Molé (1842) in good state, & entertained as became his rank. The only personage in Paris who gave great dinners, except the Ministers & High Functionaries & Rothschilds. Thiers said to me one morning, as we were walking together in the Champs Elysées, 'As for French politics, they are simple. I am 47, M. Guizot is 57, & Cte. Molé is 67.'

[16]

King Louis Philippe vindicated to me one day his refusal in 1830 of the Lieutenant General of the Kingdom during the minority of the Duc of Bordeaux (Henri V). He said he would have preferred leaving France. He said if the Duc had died during the Regency, nothing would have prevented [his] being looked upon as a criminal. 'The Duc of Bordeaux would never have had a

* Disraeli's blank.

bellyache without my being denounced throughout the world as a poisoner.'

In the King's time, there never was a dinner given at the Tuileries —no matter how stately—I have seen it in the Gallery of Diana with a hundred guests—without a huge, smoking ham being placed, at a certain time, before the King. Upon this he operated like a conjuror. The rapidity & precision with which he carved it was a marvellous feat—the slices were vast but wafer-thin. It was his great delight to carve this ham—& indeed it was a wonderful performance. He told me one day, that he had learned the trick from a waiter at Bucklersbury, where he used to dine once at an eating-house for 9d. per head. One day he called out to an honest Englishman, that he was going to send him a slice of ham, & the honest Englishman, some Consul, if I recollect right, who had been kind to the King, in America, in the days of his adversity, not used to Courts replied, that he would rather not take any. The King drew up & said 'I did not ask you whether you would take any; I said I would send you some.' A little trait, but characteristic of the dash of the Grand Seigneur, which I often observed latent in Louis Philippe, though from his peculiar temperament, & his adventurous life of strange vicissitude, he was peculiarly deficient, as his faithful & devoted friend General Baudrand often observed, in dignity—'C'est que le Roi manque—c'est la dignité.' This was a not infrequent observation in the mouth of one who, though the son of a peasant, was the most naturally dignified man I ever came across.

I shall never forget my first visit to Claremont after the catastrophe of 1848. I shrunk from it, but it was impossible to be avoided. If there were an occasion, in which one should show respectful sympathy, this was one. The family were fairly settled at Claremont when it was made.

A fine day. I went down by the railroad & got out at Esher, & then drove over to Claremont, visited for the first time. The scene was fair. I was shown into a handsome chamber, which served as a waiting room, where I found a distinguished man with whom I was acquainted,* but whose name at the moment I am writing (1863), I cannot recall. He also had come from London by

* '(q? General Fox?)': Disraeli's superscription.

appointment. We had met together at the Tuileries, & of course
we had enough to talk about, & we conversed for some little
time. Then General Dumas came into the room, & taking me
aside, said the King wished to see General Fox first, as otherwise
his impending audience would interfere with our conversation.
I bowed, & General Fox left the room with General Dumas.

I was about another quarter of an hour alone, when I was summoned; & ushered into a drawing room, where there were groups
of gentlemen. The King, who was standing, & speaking to
General Fox, who was taking his leave, then advanced, & bowed
to me with some dignity, asked some ordinary questions, in a
friendly tone. A strange question he asked was, whether I was
thinking of paying a visit to Paris—quite in an ordinary tone.
Then H.M. approached me quite closely & said in a clear but
hushed voice, 'If you will follow me, Mr Disraeli, we shall be able
to converse together undisturbed.' So we quitted the room, &
then the King led the way down a passage, which at the end was
rather gloomy, & there was a door open, & all I saw was a common mahogany glass on a painted table—& it was a bed-room, a
very ordinary one, very gloomy, looking on the walls of back
premises—but apparently the King's bed room, & then he sate
down in a small painted rush-bottomed bedroom chair, & at the
same time placed one for me exactly opposite & close to him &
without any further preface said in French, which he spoke the
whole time, 'I am desirous of telling you how all this happened.'
And then he began a narrative, which commenced with the
beginning, & never ceased until he had quitted the Tuileries an
abdicated monarch. I am sure I am understating when I say, that
the narrative considerably exceeded an hour. During this time,
the King never paused, never hesitated. He spoke with volubility
—not apparently with much feeling. He rarely looked at me as
he spoke. He seemed to me to be making a clean breast of it, &
speaking as it were to the Reporters.

I concluded from his narrative, that the whole thing was a
surprise; an accident. And that Lagrange & the secret societies,
finding everything in disorder, & no master, rose suddenly at the
eleventh hour when they found the ball was at their feet.

At last it ended; the impetus was arrested; the excitement which
had carried on the King was over & he went into hysterics. I have
seldom felt more distressed. It was a position in which one could

not even speak. Feeling deeply for this kind-hearted & clever man, who in his great prosperity, & when I was young & little known, had showered many kindnesses upon me, I with respectful tenderness took his Majesty's hand & pressed it to my lips. He took my hand & held it in both of his own. Then he rose, & in his usual voice, said 'Now, I will take you to the Queen.'

So he led me into a Drawing-room where I found the Queen working at embroidery with some ladies. General Dumas & some other attendants were standing in the background. The King presented me as if it were the Tuileries; quite cheerful. Her Majesty received me without the slightest embarrassment, with cordiality & sweet serenity, & asked me after my wife. After a short conversation, I preparing to go, the King came up & made some enquiry after Lord George Bentinck, who had spoken with sympathy & respect of the King in the House of Commons recently, & began talking of his uncle Lord William whom he had known in Sicily. Then he went on in a rather rambling way about some papers which he had which he thought might be interesting to Lord George. Of course, I assented. Whereupon the King, just as if he were at the Tuileries called for General Dumas, & gave orders, that copies should be prepared of certain documents & sent to Lord George Bentinck without loss of time.

I was told afterwards that the papers, like all other public papers, were not at Claremont, & that the King was in the habit of giving his orders on all subjects to his aides-de-camp just as if he were at Paris or St Cloud.

[17]

Mem. of Breakfast at Monckton Milnes', the only one I ever attended & why? Because he came to me & said Ibrahim Pacha who was then in England was going to breakfast with him, & he had requested his Highness to make a list of those he wished to meet him, & he had put down my name among those who had visited Egypt &c &c. I believe a fudge, but having refused M. M. 1000 times, hating breakfasting out & he very urgent, I agreed. Went late, (½ past 11 perhaps) as his breakfasts were 10 o'clockers, but kept up at the house. All the breakfast eaten; that nothing— as I never eat in public at that time. Some coffee on a disordered table; M. M. murmured something about a cutlet, not visible—which I did not notice.

Strange scene. Ibrahim not there—but Suleiman Pacha—the Revenge Frenchman (Col. Sève I think) & some Egyptian grandees. They were fighting the battle of Konieh (I think) like Corporal Trim. 'Voilà la Cavalerie' said Suleiman & he placed a spoon. 'L'infanterie est là' & he moved a coffee cup &c &c. D'Orsay standing behind him & affecting immense interest in order to make the breakfast go off well. A round table: at the fire place, Milnes' father; a Shandean squire, full of humor & affectation & astonished at the scene, not accustomed to in Yorkshire. Cobden there: a whitefaced man whom I did not know, who turned out to be Kinglake—then the author of *Eothen* which I had not read & never have, & other celebrities.

I declined to sit down, but watched the battle, & was regretting I had come, when someone touched me on the back. I looked round. It was Prince Louis Napoleon. 'Are you very much interested in this?' he said.

'Not at all; for I am neither the Conqueror nor the conquered.'

'Come here then' & he invited me to the recess of a window.

'Have you any news from Paris?' he asked me with earnest enquiry—excited.

'None, Sir.'

'Then I tell you the most important. 2000 (two thousand) Sous Lieutenants have signed a document that they will not rest until the family Buonaparte are restored to the Throne.'

'That indeed, Sir, is most important' & I thought I was talking to a madman. I believe it now to have been quite true.*

* Notation scribbled below: 'This was after Ham.'

III

THE POLITICS OF PROTECTION

18

The Clergyman &c came to the old Duke of Cambridge at Kew to suggest that there should be prayers for rain, the drought being excessive. 'By all means, by all means' he said 'but I'd be damned if you get any rain till the wind changes.'

Sir R. Peel, who refused to take office in 1839 when he might have come in comparatively unpledged, was eager in 1840 when the government tried to mitigate the monopolies, & proposed to reduce duties on corn, timber, &c, &c. There was of course a great outcry, & an outcry to be met by an exhausted Ministry. Peel was eager: almost the only time I remember him excited. 'We have the country with us' he was in the habit of saying.
   This did not indicate much foresight.

19

When I was establishing a reputation by attacking Peel—1845— or perhaps 1846—Colquhoun, who had a look to the leadership of the party—which with his views was to have been ultra Protestant as well as Protectionist—alarmed at my success, began to assume the same line—& one evening came down with a prepared harangue on both heads. Macaulay was asked what he thought of it? He replied 'Disraeli diluted.'

Great expectations were once formed of Colquhoun. He was a red-man, slender, a little above the middle size, with a sinister countenance but a high character—an Oriel first-class man. A calm, neat, bitter, terse speaker, with a distinct, though not a

powerful voice. His first efforts in Parliament had been very
successful. He had been in [in] the early Reform times as a Liberal
but returned to it after an absence of three years in 1837 as a converted Conservative, 'anxious only for the diffusion of the
Gospel' & believing Sir Robert Peel to be the very prophet of the
Lord. He was made a great deal of during the four years' campaign
of 1837 to 41—courted, petted, consulted by all Sir Robt. P's
creatures, especially Sir Geo. Clerk, himself a Scotchman. But [he]
was not provided for at the crash, on account of the very violence
of opinion which had made him inestimable in opposition at that
time when England had got very Protestant. Colquhoun never
pardoned Peel, & thought he had his opportunity of revenge at
the Maynooth grant in 1844, but Peel baffled him then. Colq. was
not equal to the situation. His chagrin was not mitigated or sustained by the inspiration of genius, & he retired from Parliament
& took refuge in religious politics—ruling supreme in Exeter
Hall—their cleverest man & their only scholar.

When he was talked of a great deal in the House of Commons
1838–40 Lytton Bulwer always in a restless fever when a man of
great expectations appeared called him to me 'The Tory Roebuck'.

[20]

Sir Robert Inglis was in appearance a medi-oval Abbot. Rather
above the middle size, very corpulent, & very rosy. His glowing
features were regular, & his eyes twinkled with voluptuous self
complacency. But there was no intellectual, or elevated, expression
in the countenance, which was not devoid of slyness. He was
elaborately polite; quite a Sir Charles Grandison, & always had
a magnificent flower in his buttonhole: something very large &
very bright; a huge rose, or a gigantic carnation, or a bunch of
geraniums. He was a wretched speaker; an offensive voice, no
power of expression, yet perpetually recalling, & correcting, his
cumbersome & wearisome phraseology.

He brought forward once a case of grievance of some prisoner,
whose wife was not permitted to visit him in prison with free
ingress & egress. He said 'Things have come to a pretty pass in
this country when an Englishman may not have his wife back-
wards & forwards.'

The shout of laughter in the House was electrical. Sir Robert Peel, who was naturally a hearty laugher, entirely lost his habitual self-control, & leant down his head in convulsions.

I have only seen him once more overpowered in that way, & that was when Bickham Escott quoted three octavo pages & a half of Tacitus—(literally) like a boy at Winchester (which he had been) at speeches. On this occasion, Peel, who had been quiet & demure for nearly a page, at last gave way. I sate behind him. I thought his life in danger. The vessels of his forehead became swollen. He at length leant over the back of the Treasury bench in a fit of risibility.

[21]

George Smythe, apropos of the Bulgarians, said of the Sclavonians 'What an unfortunate race, that have given names to the two most infamous conditions of humanity—Slaves & ——'.

A day or two after Peel's death, Gladstone was at the Carlton, & said 'Peel died at peace with all mankind; even with Disraeli. The last thing he did was to cheer Disraeli. It was not a very loud cheer, but it *was* a cheer; it was distinct. I sate next to him.'

I had concluded the great debate on the Greek (Pacifico) business, at four o'clock in the morning. It was the first, & the only time, in which the Protectionist party, acting again with Sir Robert Peel, or rather he acting again with them, I had to assume, & fulfil, the duties of leader in his presence. I wished to avoid it, as I thought it might be distressing to him, & I shrink from anything presumptuous. I had means of communicating with him, through Forbes Mackenzie, who was one of my whips & who had been a Lord of the Treasury under Peel. Though Mackenzie had resigned his office on the Repeal of the Corn Laws, he still maintained his friendly relations with Sir R. Peel & his old colleagues. Sir Robert answered Mackenzie, that he certainly meant to speak, but had no wish to close the debate. And he thought that Mr Disraeli, from his position, ought to close it.

The majority in favor of Lord Palmerston was unexpectedly large: 45. Mackenzie went to tell Sir Robert the numbers before they were declared. Sir Robert looked disappointed, & said 'I had thought it would not have exceeded 20.' I heard this myself, for in that strange state of affairs, I was only removed on the front bench, by two persons from Peel, during the latter years of his life. He was very conciliatory to me. Partly because his was not a nature that bore *rancune*; partly because, as he esteemed success in the House of Commons the greatest of human possessions, he respected a triumphant adversary; & partly, as I know, because he wished to bring back his followers into office under Lord Derby by an arrangement, which would have, of course, omitted himself.

Lord Aberdeen had planned the attack on Palmerston, under the inspiration of Madame Lieven & Guizot. The Court who attributed the fall of the Orleanist family to Lord Palmerston were favorable to it. Lord Derby had readily fallen into the scheme & had brought forward the motion of censure in the House of Lords himself, to cancel the ill effects of which Mr Roebuck's counter motion in the House of Commons had been brought forward. Lord Aberdeen, of course, would have been Secretary for Foreign Affairs. There was all reasonable room for the other Peelites, for Lord Derby had at that moment no men with pretensions to Cabinet office, except old Herries & myself. Indeed, his difficulty would have been to have had sufficient friends of his own in his own Cabinet—& perhaps Peel, or at any rate, the Peelites, saw all this, & looked upon him only as a stopgap.

The great difficulty would have been the Leadership of the House of Commons. I was the Leader of 250 men, & so far as numbers were concerned, no one could compete with me; but I not only had no official experience of high office, but I had positively never held even the humblest office. There was no confidential intimacy at that time between Lord Derby & myself; & I don't think he would have much hesitated in suggesting a Peelite, one of his old & even recent colleagues, as Leader, if I consented, & the party generally. But who? Gladstone, though he had made a capital speech in the Pacifico debate, & had stamped himself on the House as a man with a future, had certainly not then, without a party, the sufficient position. Lord Lincoln (Duke of Newcastle) & Sidney Herbert had only just got out of the egg. I have always thought, that old Goulburn was the man whom Sir Robt. Peel & Lord Derby (then Stanley?) would have brought forward, & furbished up like an old piece of dusty furniture, under whom we might have all served without any great outrage of personal feelings. But I never could penetrate this. The majority however dispelled their dreams. It was caused by a section of the Tories, who saw through the affair & looked upon it as a plot to bring the Peelites back, & put them at the head of the party, & they acted accordingly.

Next morning Peel was dead, or as good! He seemed quite well in the House, & spoke well—with none of the bitterness of his followers against Palmerston. (By the bye, Lord Palmerston met me shortly after the debate & said 'You & Peel treated me like gentlemen, which no one else did.')

Although he could not have been in bed before 5 o'clock, devoted to the Prince, he rose early to attend a Council about the projected 'Great Exhibition'. There was some financial question. He took it up, but not with his usual lucidity. Then he put pen to paper, but seemed confused, & finally said, he would think over the matter, & send his results to the Prince. He went home, & afterwards went out to ride, & it happened. Was it a fit? If so, it was brought on by unnecessary want of rest & repose. I know, as well as most men, what it is to get home at 4 or 5 in the morning after an exciting division. Sleep is not commanded, under such circumstances, even by the philosophical. Had Peel taken his fair rest, would he have been saved? Bulwer Lytton thought not, when we talked over these matters. 'He had done his work,' he said. 'No man lives, who has done his work. There was nothing left for him to do.'

I did not rise, that fatal day, so early as Sir Robert Peel. And in the afternoon, my guardian angel persuaded me, instead of going to Clubs & House of Commons, to take a drive in our agreeable environs. We were returning through the Regent's Park & two gentlemen on horseback, strangers, stopped our carriage.

'Mr Disraeli' they said. 'You will be interested to hear, that Sir Robert Peel has been thrown from his horse, & has been carried home in a dangerous state.'

'Dangerous?' I enquired. 'I hope not. His loss would be a great misfortune for this country.'

They seemed a little surprised, but I spoke what I felt.

[22]

We had been up at the House till five o'clock in the morning, & had divided on the Pacifico question. I was too tired to go to the House the next day, & took a country drive with my wife. Coming home through the Regents Park, two gentlemen on horseback, strangers, rode up to the carriage, & informed me, that Sir Robert Peel had been thrown from his horse, & was thought in danger. I bowed & said 'It was a great misfortune for the country.'

Next day, (it might be the day after), Peel still lying on his couch, there was a great morning fête at Rosebank; a thatched cottage on the banks of the Thames surrounded by groves of the flowers which gave it a name; & where to render the romantic simplicity complete, Lady Londonderry, in a colossal conservatory, condescended to make tea, from a suite of golden pots, & kettles.

Lord Londonderry was restless & absorbed: he foresaw the revolution, which the death of Peel might occasion in parties. He pressed my hand with affectionate anxiety, asked many questions, & full of intrigue, showed, as usual, his cards. I missed him during the fête. He reappeared towards the end. He came up, & whispered to me. It was hopeless. He had actually galloped up to London, called at Whitehall, & galloped back again, while his band was still playing, & his friends still sipping ices.

Sir Francis Burdett was a very high bred man, very tall, & with a distinguished countenance. He was a complete Norman. As an orator, in his best days, he had no equal. It was all grace & music; never was a more commanding manner or a finer voice. The range of his subjects was limited, referring mainly to the character of the constitution; & the rights & grievances of the people &c &c, but of these he was master. His declamation was fiery & thrilling, but always natural. He was one of the most natural speakers I recollect, never betrayed into bombast, either in matter or manner. He had considerable power of sarcasm & his hits always told. His quotations were, I think, generally from Shakespeare.

In politics, he was a Jacobite. He was sprung from a Jacobite family & entered life with the hereditary opinions of his class. He was against the Boromongers, that is to say, the new Capitalist classes which Wm the 3d & the House of Hanover had introduced: he was for annual Parliaments & universal suffrage, as Sir William Wyndham & Sir John Hinde Cotton had been before him, in order to curb & control these classes. The latter (also Sir J. Cotton) was for the ballot. It so happened, that the French Revolution was coincident with Burdett's appearance in public life, & so in the confusion of circumstances it turned out, that he was looked upon as a Jacobin, when in reality he was a Jacobite.

The English Public which is particularly ignorant of history joined in the taunts of his inconsistency, when, late in life, the Boromongers having been got rid of, Burdett turned out to be what he started [as], a high aristocratic English Politician.

He was extremely vain, but not offensively so; his high breeding prevented that: & under all circumstances, he was distinguished by simplicity.

I think he was the greatest gentleman I ever knew.

For many years after he entered Parliament he rode up to Westminster from his seat in Wiltshire on horseback. The country, especially in that part of England, was then very open, & abounded in downs & commons.

In one of his last speeches in Parliament, (then reformed, & full of quiet middle class people) on the expenses of elections, he greatly denounced them, & observed that he had a right to give an opinion on this subject, as there was a period in his life, when parliamentary contests had reduced him to a state of absolute beggary. There was a murmur of admiring incredulity. 'I assure you Sir,' he continued, 'I am indulging in no exaggeration. Honourable gentlemen may not believe it, but I can assure them there was a time, when Lady Burdett had only one pair of horses to her carriage!'

The effect of this remark in one of the early reformed Parliaments full of retired tradesmen, many of whom had amassed wealth, but had never plucked up courage to keep a carriage, may be conceived. It was the most patrician definition of poverty ever made.

He was very goodnatured, especially to young members—but rather absent, & thoughtless in domestic arrangements. He would say to me (1838 & so on) 'Will you take your mutton with me today? We are quite alone. Come in boots. You won't be wanted for an hour.' And I often went. He lived in St James's Place. His dinners were most agreeable. Lady Burdett, a clever woman, but a great invalid, appeared after dinner—& there were several agreeable daughters. One day he asked me to take mutton, & so on, & when I arrived in frock, I was ushered into illumined saloons, full of grand guests in full *tenue*!

When he was taunted at the beginning of 1837 (I think) with changing his opinions, he gallantly resigned the seat for Westminster, & declared himself at the same time, a candidate for the vacancy. It was a crisis in the Conservative Cause, & was generally felt on both sides that his fate would decide the future course of politics. The Tories worked hard. The Carlton Club mapped the city into districts, & divided them among the ardent youth of the party. May-Fair fell to me & Sir Robert Pigot, & very great fun we had. There was one street in our district entirely filled with cooks, chiefly Foreigners. Ten years afterwards, writing *Tancred*, I availed myself of the experience then obtained, & it formed my first chapter.

Burdett won his election—& no one ever enjoyed a triumph more. Perhaps he found the contest still more exciting. He was 'at home' every evening during it, in his dining room, & all might come who cared. There he delivered every evening one of his constitutional harangues, or invectives against O'Connell then in the Liberal ascendant. They were very fiery & created great enthusiasm when he denounced the manner of the famous agitator 'half bully, & half blarney'.

[23]

In 1849 there was a grand dinner given in Merchant Taylors' Hall to inaugurate the new organisation of the 'Protectionist Party' under the Leadership of Lord Derby & myself. Tom Baring was in the chair. On his right Lord Derby, myself on his left, & then there were alternately Peers & Commoners. The Duke of Northumberland, whom I did not then know, was to have sate next to me—but His Grace was unwell & prevented attending at the last moment. The Commoner next to His Grace's seat was Mr Croker. He was requested by the Directors of the Fête to sit up next to me. It was rather embarrassing. But Mr Croker & myself were not socially acquainted. I had never seen him since I was a boy. Nor was he the person, who ought to assume, that a character in one of my books, which he deemed odious, was intended for himself. He behaved like a man of the world: informed me that he had had the pleasure of he hoped the friendship of my excellent father, talked generally about the political situation, warmed into anecdote, & made himself agreeable. I treated him with great consideration, & spoke enough, but not too much, & took care never to break into cordiality, which I should have done under ordinary circumstances with so eminent [a] man, met under such conditions.

When I made my speech after dinner, I observed he nodded his head frequently in approbation, & gave other signs of sympathy & perhaps stronger feeling. I thought all this on his part a very good performance & that he had extricated himself out of an embarrassing position with dexterity & some grace.

A year or two afterwards—I think 1850—it might be February of 1851—but I had brought forward a great agricultural motion on the burthens of land, had rallied great numbers, had been beaten by the government in a full House, by only 15 or 16 votes or even less—had made a great statement at the commencement of the debate which lasted some days, & had concluded it by a brilliant reply which made much noise at the time & was doubly effective from the capital division that followed. I was standing in the Hall of the Carlton, which was rather full—reading a letter—when a person came up to me & put his hand on my arm & said 'The speech was the speech of a Statesman, & the reply was the reply of a Wit.' It was Croker.

I was surprised, & murmured something* about 'laudari a laudato' but he had vanished. He had too much good taste to remain. Years after this, George Smythe brought me, one morning, a letter from Croker, who had long been hopelessly ill, to his father Lord Strangford—(Camoens) with whom Croker had been at College & always chums—& this letter, if it meant anything, meant a formal reconciliation with me—it seemed even an inter-

---

* Disraeli's original ending for this sentence, which he crossed out, revealed all too clearly his animosity towards Croker: 'about "laudari a laudato viro" but as George Smythe said "It must have stuck in my throat, because everybody thought Croker very clever but nobody ever praised him".'

view. I remember in the letter this passage. 'Why he attacked me I never could discover, & know no more the cause, than I know the man, who shot Mr. Hampden!'

I behaved as kindly as I could under the circumstances—but I could not listen to interviews, or reconciliations, or explanations. It was too late—& my sensibilities which had [been] played upon in my earlier life too much required nursing. I told George Smythe to manage the result with the greatest consideration for Croker's feelings & situation—& there it ended.

The moral I draw from all this is that men of a certain age like the young ones, who lick them. I think, now, that Croker was quite sincere at the Merchant Taylors'. And I observed this also in Peel. He sate almost next to me during the last years of his Parliamentary life. It was an odd arrangement but inevitable. I was Leader of the Opposition, & therefore sate opposite the Red-Box on the left hand of the Speaker—Peel was leader of the late government, & almost entitled to the same place. I had recourse to many little arts to spare his feelings, & to get fellows to sit between us & all that—but he never assisted me in these endeavours; quite the reverse—& I have since more than once suspected, that he meant to make our respective positions in the House a means of gradually bringing about a reconciliation. In one of my great 'Protectionist' motions as they were called though I carefully avoided advocating Protectionism in them, which he was obliged to oppose, he took elaborate pains to assure the House, looking at me the whole time, that he bore no enmity to any member on account of former struggles & differences of opinion. His language was so cordial & his manner so marked, that it was much cheered by his own friends, & all the men of sense of [my] own party—as indicating ultimate fusion on honorable terms.

There were other traits & circumstances I could mention, & as Gladstone said, he died cheering me.

Croker, Peel, & O'Connell sent me, I may say, messages of peace before they died. Literally O'Connell. He was so delighted with my smashing of Peel, & so glad, perhaps, that he had escaped what I once threatened & he now found I could do, that he sent me a message that it had always been heavy on his heart, that there should have been a misunderstanding between us, & that he had long known that he had been misinformed & misled in the matter. I sent him a very courteous reply: but avoided any personal communication. He always made me a very reverential bow afterwards.

After my great speech in 1846 on the second reading of the Bill for the Repeal of the Corn Laws, & which was followed by the loudest & the longest cheer that ever was heard in the House of Commons, a gentleman who was obliged to be a Protectionist, but no friend of mine, but very much of Sir R. Peel, met O'Connell in the Lobby & asked him what he thought of my speech.

'I should have said' replied the great Dan 'that it was one of the ablest speeches I ever heard in the House of Commons, but for the Invective—' 'Ah!' said the Protectionist shaking his head & looking quite mournful at the mention of the sacrilege. 'But for the invective' continued O'Connell '& that made it incomparable.'

'What a sell!' said Lord March who heard it & came & told me.

[24]

This coup d'état, as Bankes called it, rendered an immediate conference between Lord Derby & myself necessary. There could be no doubt that the Queen would send for him: in fact there was no other person. There had been long a House of Commons rumor, that the Protectionists must try their hand. My agricultural divisions had brought it to this pass. Again, the eternal question, how was a Government to be formed? Lord Derby thought he could manage sufficiently in the House of Lords, but at all times, when a party was rich in patrician states-men, it was unwise to rest too much on the House of Lords for the materials of a Ministry. Said he thought that 'Malmesbury would make a good Colonial Secretary.' Reducing it to a mini-mum, to be excused only by the extraordinary circumstances of the case, it was impossible to meet Parliament with less than six Cabinet Ministers on the front bench of the House of Commons; it ought to be eight. It did not appear that from our own resources we could furnish more than three men—Herries, Lord Granby & myself, & of these three only one had any official experience, & though an able man was worn out, & the intended Leader of the House not only never having been in office, but with very little parliamentary experience. Mr Disraeli had been ten years in

Parliament from 1837 to 47 & never been placed on any Committee & it was only during the four subsequent years, that he had had any opportunity of making himself in any degree acquainted with the multifarious duties of a leading member of the House of Commons.

It was evident, that Lord Derby was sanguine of a fusion with the Peelites & of the revival of the old connection. They sate (even Graham) on the opposition benches; they were a staff without an army; it seemed a necessary & a natural solution. Graham had paid me a marked tribute in debate: Gladstone had supported my motion & voted with me. Mr Disraeli was very much in favor of such an arrangement, & always encouraged it. But he was not sanguine as to the result. The difficulty was the Leadership of the Commons. It was impossible, that the Colleagues of Sir R. Peel, veteran & even illustrious statesmen, could be led by one, who had stepped out of the ranks, had destroyed their famous leader, & covered them with confusion. For this reason from the first, Mr D. not only expressed his readiness to waive his claims, but impressed upon Lord Derby the necessity of such conduct on his part. Lord Derby, perhaps from delicacy or consideration for Mr D's feelings never reciprocated this feeling. Indeed he once said, that he had no idea, that the man who had brought things to this point, should not reap the great reward. But the truth is, the difficulty was one which could not be removed by individual sacrifice. The Protectionist party, though they were prepared (, though not very willingly,) to accept the services of the Peelites in a subaltern position made it a condition sine qua non, that the Ministry should be led in both Houses by their own chiefs. Irrespective of the Protectionist quarrel, the Peelites were very unpopular at this moment in the country on account of the line they had taken respecting the Papacy.

Lord Derby, evidently indisposed towards Graham, & neither desirous, nor sanguine, of any arrangement with him, was still more than hopeful, that he should obtain Gladstone, & that G. by his influence & management, would obtain sufficient aid from his friends to give us in the present state of parties, a working majority. Still it was necessary, with the royal audience impending, to contemplate the possibility of having to form a government from our own resources, & ultimately I proposed to Lord Derby three names, in addition to the preceding ones, who I thought might be reputably introduced to Parliament as advisers of the Crown. These names were

Sir Robert Inglis, whom I proposed for the India Board; Mr. Henley who, I observed, had obtained a certain position in the House; & Mr. Henry Corry, who had been Secretary of the Admiralty under Sir Robert Peel, had the reputation of a good administrator & always addressed the house on the duties of his department with fluency, clearness, & a knowledge of his subject.

Lord Derby shrugged his shoulders, but made no difficulties, which was not his way.

We parted, & I think it was in the evening, that I received a note from Lord Derby informing me, that he had been summoned by Her Majesty to Buckingham Palace early on the following morning, & should call on me immediately after his audience.

Accordingly he called at Grosvenor Gate, early, I should think by noon, & came up stairs to me in the blue room. His face was radiant, his eye merry as he entered, & he said raising as was his custom, his mocking eyebrows 'Well, we are launched!' And then he became serious 'I have not kissed hands' he said 'but I have promised the Queen, that I would try to form a government.'

To effect this object, [he] had informed H.M. that he would appeal for assistance to the followers of the late Sir Robert Peel, & that with that view was willing that the question of Protection should be an open one until the Country by a dissolution should have had the opportunity of giving its opinion upon it. He told me, that Her Majesty had enquired of him to whom he proposed to entrust the Leadership of the House of Commons? & he had mentioned my name.

The Queen said 'I always felt, that if there were a Protectionist Government, Mr Disraeli must be the Leader of the House of Commons but I do not approve of Mr Disraeli. I do not approve of his conduct to Sir Robert Peel.'

Lord Derby said 'Madam, Mr Disraeli has had to make his position, & men who make their positions will say & do things, which are not necessary to be said or done by those for whom positions are provided.'

'That is true' said the Queen '& all I can now hope is, that having attained this great position, he will be temperate. I accept Mr Disraeli on your guarantee.'

'And now' said Lord Derby 'I am going to write to Gladstone to call on me. Be with me late in the afternoon to know the result & consult.'

The interview between Lord Derby & G. was entirely unsuccessful. No question arose as to the formation* of the Government, or as to leadership of the House. Gladstone would not listen to Protection being an open question: he required an absolute renunciation of that policy; a specific declaration, that the new Government completely accepted it—*un fait accompli*. Lord Derby was in good spirits. He told me that he had written to Sir Stratford Canning at Constantinople to offer him the Secy. for F.O. of which I greatly approved, & to the Duke of Northumberland—the Admiralty than which nothing could be better. In fact, Lord Derby was full of resource, which was not his characteristic. 'I have written' he said 'to Ellenborough, & Lord Lonsdale, President of the Council, to Sir Robert Inglis, Henley, & Henry Corry, as you advise, to call on me tomorrow—& of course Herries & Granby. You be with me early, after breakfast.'

When I called the next morning accordingly, he was in high spirits. He said 'An answer from the Duke of Northumberland accepting; Inglis has been with me & accepted. Ellenborough is to be here in $\frac{1}{2}$ an hour. No other answers.' Malmesbury was to be Secy. for the Col., Canning for the F.O. & myself, Leader of the H of C. & Home; Herries C. of Exr., Henley Bd. of Trade; Inglis, India, & the Duke of Northumberland—a great card—Admy.—Lord Lonsdale President—things did not look very bad. They were showy, but after all, the great thing was the House of Commons & that was not settled.

While we were talking—in the library at his first house in St. James's Square (now Tollemache's)—Lord Ellenborough was announced. He was, I think, to have been Privy Seal, but it never came to mentioning office to him. I would have retired, but Lord Derby told me to go into his Dressing-room, that was adjoining, on the same floor, a spacious apartment, & conceal myself. In about half an hour, I heard a merry shout 'Come out from your dungeon!'

He was so gay, that I was hopeful—but no! the mighty Earl had refused. On the same grounds, almost the same words as Gladstone. 'Never mind' said Lord Derby. 'It's the House of

* Disraeli wrote 'materials' above.

Commons we must look after' & almost as he was speaking, the Groom of the Chambers announced Mr Henry Corry in attendance. I returned to my dungeon, but was not kept there very long.

Henry Corry had not absolutely fainted, but had turned very pale when the proposition was made to him of becoming a leading member of a Protectionist Government, & had declined what, as Lord Derby said, under no conceivable circumstances, a year ago could ever have been offered to him, & which never can be offered again. Lord Derby was a little more serious, but still up to the mark. 'With Canning' he said 'we have still six Cabinet Ministers in the Commons.'

At two o'clock which was now approaching, there was to be a general meeting; Lord Lonsdale, Lord Malmesbury, Lord Granby, Beresford (Chief Whip), Sir Edward Sugden, who had accepted the Chancellorship & some others. Herries & Henley, who were also to have attended but who were to have called previously, had never arrived. Just as the servant had informed Lord Derby, that these personages were assembled, a letter arrived from Sir Robert Inglis, withdrawing his assent. Lord Derby's countenance fell.

However, he came in & addressed his friends with cheerfulness & dignity (Henley had arrived). He told them that the Queen, as they were aware, had sent for him; that he had undertaken to try to form a government; that he had applied to Mr Gladstone & his friends but they refused, unless Protection was unequivocally relinquished; that we were therefore thrown on our own resources; that he had written to Sir Stratford Canning to accept the Foreign Office—& that Lord Lonsdale who had consented to be President of Council, had kindly agreed to transact the duties of F.O. until Canning arrived; that the Duke of Northumberland had consented to be First Lord of Admiralty; that Lord Malmesbury was [to] be Secretary of State for Colonies; that what he wanted was official support in the House of Commons, that he felt confident, that I would completely discharge the duties of Leader of that House; that he was sure the country would be satisfied if Finance were entrusted to the experienced hands of Mr Herries, whose unexpected absence he regretted; that Lord Granby would take a place in the Cabinet; that he hoped their friend Mr Henley could consent to become President of the Board of Trade; that he had counted on the assistance of one or two

more in the House of Commons but had been disappointed, &
now should like to hear their general views on the matter. Lord
Lonsdale followed like a man of the world; said it was not a time
to make difficulties; the Whigs were prostrate; we must support
Lord Derby; he would be provisional Secretary of State.

All this time, Henley, whom I believe Lord Derby did not
personally know, or scarcely, sate on a chair against the dining-
room wall, leaning with both his hands on an ashen staff, & with
the countenance of an ill-conditioned Poor Law Guardian cen-
sured for some act of harshness. His black eye brows, which met,
deeply knit, his crabbed countenance doubly morose, but no
thought in the face, only ill-temper, perplexity & perhaps
astonishment. In the midst of this, Herries was ushered, or rather
tumbled, into the room, exclaiming 'What's all this?' Then there
were explanations how, & why, he had not received a letter, &
had not been there at 12 o'clock in the morning, to know that he
was to be Chancellor of the Exchequer.

If Henley were mute & grim, without a word, suggestion, or
resource, Herries, who had had considerable experience of official
life to my great surprise was as unsatisfactory in a different
manner. He was garrulous, & foresaw only difficulties. He
seemed to be full of fear of Goulburn, who was to do this, & to
prevent that, & in short render the administration of the finances
by a follower of Lord Derby an impossibility. We none of us then
knew much about finance, but the impression that Herries, who
was deemed a great judge in such matters, contrived to convey,
was that our monetary affairs were in a critical state, & that
Goulburn would eat us up alive if we presumed to touch them.
It turned out afterwards that no difficulties of moment existed, but
by postponing our government we insured—as for instance in the
matter of the Income Tax.

When Henley spoke at last, he flatly refused to take the Board
of Trade—& being a very suspicious man, it came out afterwards
as Herries told me, that he thought there was some sort of con-
spiracy to throw all the difficulties of the government on himself
& Herries, who would have had to fight the battle of the revised
Tariff, which these profound statesmen were to introduce to
counteract the free trade measures.

Lord Derby & myself exchanged looks, & I pretty well understood what was passing in his mind. Lord Malmesbury suggested

some other place to Henley, murmured something about the India Board; Lord Lonsdale tried to soften him into an approach to the manners of civilised society. There was something like the general chatter of a club-room, when Lord Derby made a sign to me, & we withdrew to the end of the room.

'This will never do?' he said.

'I am not sanguine—but don't be in a hurry.'

After a few remarks on the extraordinary scene, he returned to the table. There was silence, & he gave it as his opinion, that it was his duty to decline the formation of a government, &, particularly, from his inability to find members of the House of Commons who were prepared to co-operate with him.

Sir Edward Sugden, though he lost a peerage, agreed with Lord Derby; Lord Lonsdale seemed disappointed, Malmesbury distressed; Herries & Henley said nothing. Beresford frantically rushed forward & took Lord Derby aside & said there were several men, he knew, waiting at the Carlton expecting to be sent for, & implored Lord Derby to reconsider his course. Lord Derby enquired impatiently 'Who was at the Carlton?' Beresford said 'Deedes'. 'Pshaw!' exclaimed Lord Derby. 'These are not names I can put before the Queen. Well, my Lords & gentlemen, I am obliged to you for your kind attendance here today—but the thing is finished. Excuse my leaving you, but I must write to the Queen at once.'

We dispersed: lingering in the Hall, Lord Lonsdale said 'Never was such an opportunity lost. They were prostrate. We ought to have dissolved Parliament tomorrow.'

'We are f——d' said Malmy. 'The best thing the Country party can do is to go into the Country. There is not a woman in London who will not laugh at us.'

Herries, who seemed annoyed that all was over, kept mumbling about not having received his summons till three o'clock & that he remembered governments which were weeks forming. Henley continued silent & grim. Beresford looked like a man, who had lost his all at roulette, & kept declaring that he believed Deedes was a first rate man of business.

[25]

As the Government had resigned, & Lord Derby had declined, it was necessary to extricate the Court, & everybody else, from an embarrassing, & almost absurd, position, so the Queen, after sounding Lord Aberdeen (I believe) who shrank from the proffer, to act in a strictly constitutional manner, sent for the Duke of Wellington, who, of course, advised her Majesty to request her late Ministers to continue in office. After all was arranged, His Grace called on Lord Derby & talked over affairs. He evidently thought them very satisfactory for Lord Derby, & generally for his old political friends, with whom His Grace always sympathised. Thus he summed up the position 'Well! they are in the mud, & now you can look about you.'

The Duke of Wellington contemplated the re-union of the Conservative party under Lord Derby, when the next, & inevitable, crash took place—I did not take that view. The extraordinary circumstances of 1851 brought their moral to me, but it was different from the Duke of Wellington. The Whigs might be in the mud, but it was clear to me, that another party was not in a more clean predicament.

One thing was established, that every statesman* of experience & influence however slight declined to act under Lord Derby unless the principle of protection were unequivocally renounced.

In the autumn of the year 1849, when taking advantage of distress a Mr. G. F. Young & what was called the Protection Society to British Industry were agitating the country, I had made a strong effort to counteract their pernicious course, & to direct the public attention to more practical measures of relief in the remission of taxation, than the frantic reaction they advocated, & which I was convinced no great class in the country itself either desired or deemed practicable.

This had brought strong remonstrances from Lord Derby, with whom my relations during the whole of the year 1849 were uneasy. He was in the hands of the Protection Society worked by this George Fredk. Young, who was not an agriculturist—but a commercial & mainly colonial interest man, ignorant of the temper & situation of the farmers, a man of great energy, & of

* 'public man' written above, and preferable in the context.

equal vanity but of ordinary abilities & no cultivation, & who was piqued by the success of Cobden & Bright, men of his own class, in agitating England & thought he would show himself as good & powerful as they. G.F. Young had got hold of Beresford, who had originally intruded himself into the office of first Whip of the Protectionist Party & was in daily communication with Lord Derby, who really saw nobody else, but him & a few companions in the House of Lords all greatly his inferiors in intellect & acquirement. Beresford was a tall, coarse man, who could blend with his natural want of refinement, if necessary, extreme servility: very persevering, capable of labor, prejudiced, & bigoted. Protection & Protestantism were his specifics for all the evils of the state, & the only foundation for strong & lasting governments. And these were the results, that he was always driving into Lord Derby's (then Lord Stanley's) ears. He persuaded Lord Derby, that they were the real sentiments of the Tory party in the House of Commons, & especially of the middle class of the country of which Beresford affected, as a man of business in his way—a Director of Banks & Insurance offices, with which he eked out a precarious income—to have peculiar knowledge.

In 1850 the relations between Lord Derby & myself had become more cordial. I had become the sole & recognised leader of the Tory party in the House of Commons & had begun to shake the Ministry by my motions on Agricultural Relief. The possibility of a 'Protectionist Government' began to be talked about. I attempted on several occasions to bring Lord Derby to bear on the subject of Protection, but I soon found that his prejudices on the subject, & his distrust of me with regard to it, were not to be easily removed.

The ludicrous catastrophe of 1851 determined me no longer to trifle with the question, & I laid before him my views, that he ought to seize the opportunity afforded by his not being able to serve his sovereign in consequence of inability to form an administration on the protective principle, publickly to relinquish that ground, so that he might be free to act with other statesmen, & thus, Sir Robert Peel being no more, place himself at the head of the re-constructed Conservative party, & also in a full & unequivocal manner impressed him with my conviction, & the grounds for that conviction, that he misapprehended the feeling of the country on the subject, & even of his own friends; & I assured him, with no mean opportunities of observation on the matter, that the agricultural classes in the main looked upon a recurrence to protection as an impossibility, & looked upon its advocacy as an obstacle to practically remedial measures. I intimated that every year, from the necessity of things, a recurrence to an abrogated policy [was] becoming more difficult, & I impressed upon him, that I already saw changes in the state of affairs, which indicated that the pressure on the land was diminishing.

With what success I laboured may be inferred from the following letter, dated Jan. 18, 1852 written apparently with some irritation, for which there was no cause, as* I had no communication whatever with the scribe to whose labors it relates.†

In the autumn of this year the expulsion of Lord Palmerston from the Cabinet had taken place—& the Government was consequently more in the 'mud' than before. All indicated a crisis on the meeting of Parliament. Lord Derby took the opportunity on the first night (I think) of its meeting in 1852 to make a declaration on the subject of Protection. I really believe, that in taking this course, he was influenced by my representations, & wished to make a declaration, that on the whole would reconcile all parties. His scheme seemed to be the adoption of the American Tariff. It appeared to me to be Protection in its most odious form —& I was without hope.

Lord Palmerston lost not a moment in moving an amendment to the first Government measure, which ensured their defeat (Militia Bill). An eager friend anticipating that he would be sent for by the Queen, would not allow Lord John Russell an opportunity of escape, but forced him to pledge himself that night to consider his Ministry finished.

* Here Disraeli originally wrote 'the Mr P in question was an impudent adventurer'.

† In this letter Derby complained that Samuel Phillips, a journalist friendly to Disraeli, had attempted to publish in the *Morning Herald* an article 'urging the necessity of the abandonment of Protection'. Phillips apparently implied that information given him by Disraeli indicated that Derby favoured this course. Derby vehemently denied that he intended 'to take office with the purpose of throwing over, voluntarily, the main object of those who have raised us to it . . .'. Hughenden Papers B/XX/S/43; also quoted, almost in full, in W. F. Monypenny and G. E. Buckle, *The Life of Benjamin Disraeli*, vol. 3 (London, 1914), pp. 316–17.

But the Court, though it disliked the Protectionists, disliked Lord Palmerston whom they had absolutely dismissed in the autumn more, & Lord Derby, to the great astonishment of Lord Palmerston's friends was again sent for.

Lord Derby was not in town; he was at the Duke of Beaufort's, at Badminton, a shooting party. I wrote to him from the House of Commons counselling him to seize the opportunity of forming a strong government—to offer the Leadership of the House of Commons to Lord Palmerston & places in the Cabinet to such friends as he desired, & to assure Lord Palmerston from me that he would find in me a loyal lieutenant. I sent off Mackenzie, the Junior Whip at once to Badminton, who arrived there the following morning—before the news of the resignation was known.

Here is Lord Derby's answer, just arrived in St James's Square.* On the previous evening, I had met Lord Palmerston at Lady Foley's. He said to me enquiringly 'Well, how long will Derby's government last? He may have it for five years?'

'I think Lord Derby's government might last more than five years, if it be properly formed' I replied. I was greatly tempted to open the subject to him at once, but from a feeling of delicacy towards Lord Derby refrained.

I saw Lord Derby before the audience. He went resolved to form a Ministry & to kiss hands. When Lord Derby informed the Queen of his intention of applying to Lord Palmerston to combine in forming a government & of offering him the Leadership of the House of Commons H.M. seemed distressed. 'If you do it' she said 'he will never rest till he is your master.'

After leaving the Queen Lord Derby had his interview with Lord Palmerston. ? Lord Derby had kissed hands which Lord Palmerston knew. What were Lord Palmerston's real intentions† at that moment, must remain a mystery. I am inclined to believe, that he might have been induced‡ to join Lord Derby. His political position was very desolate. He had no party. Not a single man of mark had followed him, when he was ignominiously ejected from office. Indeed only two individuals, & those obscure,

---

* Derby replied (21 February 1852) that, whatever happened, he would 'never forget the generous self-sacrifice offered by the note which I received by Mackenzie at Badminton this morning'. Hughenden Papers B/XX/S/48; Monypenny and Buckle, *Disraeli*, 3, 342–43.

† 'views' written above. ‡ Originally 'he was prepared'.

had expressed their determination to blend their public fate with his. Lord Derby impressed upon him, that the offer was made entirely with my sanction & that he would find me an able* loyal lieutenant. Lord Palmerston said he was quite satisfied on that head: he had no doubt of our getting on well together. With regard to friends for the Cabinet, he had none to suggest except on public grounds, equally open to Lord Derby as himself: with respect to any followers or private friends in regard to subordinate office, he had no wishes; there was nobody that he cared to provide for.

This seemed promising enough: but then came the main principles on which the Cabinet should be formed. Lord Palmerston did not think that Protection could be left an open question; that it could be left in an ambiguous position. He had no prejudices on the subject. He had always been in favor of a moderate fixed duty on foreign Corn. He had advocated it in 1846; to the very last. But it was too late to think of such things in 1852. He would be party to no Ministry which contemplated the possibility of any change or modification in the Free Trade Measures.

This ended the affair, & Lord Derby came to me from Piccadilly Terrace (Beaumont's House where the Pams then lived) at Grosvenor Gate. He would make no further overtures: in that he was wise, as it could only have been a waste of time. He recurred to my being Chancellor of the Exchequer which he had opened to me before. I had then demurred, as a branch of which I had no knowledge. He replied 'You know as much as Mr Canning did. They give you the figures.' He said then definitively that Lord Malmesbury was to be Secretary for Foreign Affairs, but nothing of his position as regarded Sir Stratford Canning. Herries, he said, must be Colonial Secretary. Henley should go to Board of Trade. Walpole, a recruit of last year, was to be Home Secretary. John Manners to be in the Cabinet, vice Granby. He must now go home at once: he had to write to the Queen, & to all these persons & many others, & begged me to be with him early on the morrow.

When I called on the morrow, I found his house already full of people: men in every room. His servant told me Mr Herries was with his Lord, & that he had enquired several times for me, & that my name was to be taken in immediately.

* Disraeli inserted 'able' as an afterthought.

A very few minutes elapsed before I was in his presence. It was rather a face of consternation. 'I really think we shall break down' he said. 'What am I to do for a Colonial Secretary?'

So, then it turned out, that Herries, evidently disgusted at not being Chancellor of Exchequer, had peremptorily refused the Secretaryship. I instantly counselled my giving up the Chancellorship, which I didn't want, but Lord Derby would not hear of it. The recollection of the scene of last year evidently influenced him: besides, he thought, that the Leader of the House of Commons should be under the same official roof as himself. What was to be done?

'I know the man' I said. 'He will do very well.'

'Who?'

'Pakington!'

'I have just sent for him to be Under Secretary to Walpole. It should be a Country gentleman. I thought it was a capital arrangement. He will be here in a few minutes.'

Sir John Pakington was announced. He remained in the waiting room, while I was convincing Lord Derby, that he would make a competent Secretary of State. It was, naturally, rather hard work. I don't know, that Lord Derby had even a personal acquaintance with Pakington at that moment. The exigency at last conquered him—he said with an almost merry face of perplexity —'Will you be bail for him?'

'To any amount' I said.

I had only a public acquaintance with Pakington, who, though obliged to vote with the Protectionists, always kept aloof & pitched up with the Peelites, for which Peel made him a Baronet. But I had observed him, especially on Lord George Bentinck's colonial committee.

Pakington was introduced, elated with the impending destiny of becoming an Under Secretary. Lord Derby explained the situation in his happiest manner. Never shall I forget Pakington's countenance, as the exact state of affairs broke upon him: never did I witness such a remarkable mixture of astonishment & self-complacency.

IV

'ALL WONDERFULLY CHANGED'

[26]

After the revolution of 1848, the favorite theory of Guizot, then an exile here was, that 'France was worn out'.

Thiers made a visit to England in 1851 & dined at my house. To meet him the present Speaker of the House of Commons, then Evelyn Denison, Lord Malmesbury, & Henry Lennox. I only asked him the day before, at the House of Commons where he was witnessing the debate—an impromptu dinner, but very agreeable. Thiers never ceased talking—& always French politics. The great question was, what was to happen when the Presidency of Louis Napoleon, then fast waning, should cease.

Thiers said, & repeatedly, 'I will not pretend to say what will happen: but I will guarantee you what will not happen. Buonaparte has no chance. He is universally rejected & despised.'

[27]

Monckton Milnes was a goodnatured fellow, & not naturally bad-hearted; he was highly instructed, & very clever. But he was always ridiculous—from an insane vanity. This excess of a sentiment, which, when limited, is only amusing, was accompanied by a degree of envy which made him unamiable.

When I published *Coningsby*, he complained to me, that I had not introduced his character among the Young England group, to which he was attached in feeling, & with whom he wished to act—& had sometimes. He spoke to me on this matter with great earnestness—tears in his eyes—I had never appreciated him, & all that sort of thing. As his father was a friend of mine, & I always

wished to be on good terms with Milnes (though George Smythe
hated him with a sort of diablerie & treated him with a fantastic
insolence which requires a great pen to picture) I at length promised, that if the opportunity offered, I would remember his wish.
Accordingly when I wrote 'Tancred' in which the Young England
group re-appeared, I sketched the character of Vavasour, & I
made it as attractive as I could consistent with that verisimilitude
which [was]* necessary. I don't know whether he was over-
satisfied—but between 1844 & 1847 when *Tancred* was published
(*Sybil* in 1845, & *Tancred* was intended for 1846—but the publication postponed in consequence of the great Corn Law Repeal)
much had happened in my position: the Young England myth
had evaporated, & I had become if not the recognised leader, at
least the most influential organ, of a powerful parliamentary party.
Milnes was full of envy.

'It is impossible, that I & Sidney Herbert' he went about saying
'can be led by Disraeli.'†

No one expected that Sidney Herbert would be led by me. He
was a member of Sir Robert Peel's Cabinet, which had been mainly,
if not entirely, destroyed by my efforts. Milnes was one of the
most insignificant members of the House of Commons—but he
gratified his vanity by classing in his own talk himself with S.
Herbert.

In Easter 1846, when the success of Peel was doubtful, Milnes,
who had not a rural taste or accomplishment, came up from
Yorkshire after the recess in a Squire's cutaway green coat, with
basket buttons. As he entered the House, G. Smythe exclaimed
'See Dicky—Protection looking up.'

When he found that Peel was flung in a ditch, he changed his
politics, & took to Palmerston, whom, as well as Lady Palmerston, he toadied with a flagrant perseverance that made every one
smile. His passion was office. He wanted to sit on the Treasury
bench, with folded arms, & to be a man of business. Palmerston
was ready to do anything for him except give him office—&
refused him everything on every occasion. He always went to
relieve his feelings & plead his cause to Lady Palmerston who

---

* Disraeli repeated 'verisimilitude' here and omitted a verb. The slip
occurred at the turning of a page.

† This sentence originally read: 'It is quite impossible, that I & Sidney
Herbert' he said 'can follow Disraeli.'

smoothed him down, asked him to perpetual dinners, & said he was a 'social favorite'.

Sydney Smith used to call him 'the cool of the evening' when he went about to his parties. Being terribly familiar he called the great witty critic 'Sydney', who looked astounded, but said nothing at the time. Shortly afterwards Milnes very fussily regretting that he could not meet S.S. at Lady Ashburton's, because he was engaged to dine with the Archbishop of Canterbury, Sydney Smith said 'Ah! well! by the bye, let me give you a friendly hint, don't call the Archbishop*—"Howley", because, perhaps, he might not be used to it.'

Milnes' claims became at length so urgent, that Palmerston bethought himself of this device—to offer a peerage to his father. The elder Milnes was the contemporary, & had been the friend, of Palmerston. They had entered Parliament together, & there was a rumor, not I believe without foundation, that Perceval, when he was made Prime-Minister, had offered the Chancellorship of the Exchequer both to Palmerston & to Milnes, who had a 'single speech' reputation. Milnes refused this high office, & probably afterwards repented his refusal, for he retired from public life, & became a fantastic, Shandean, country-gentleman, highly instructed, & very clever—but queer & affected, as clever men dissatisfied with themselves often become.

He was a great Protectionist, & that struggle called him back for a moment to public life. He made a brilliant speech at a County Meeting, after a silence of forty years, & was one of my warmest supporters. Milnes did not dislike his son, but he was very sensible of his absurdities—& was not disinclined to teaze & mortify him a little in little things. So he refused the Peerage. There never was such blank astonishment! And Dicky was in despair. The alleged reason for refusing the peerage was, that the intended Peer was not a supporter of the Government—which as old Milnes was not in Parliament & had never interfered in any public question except Protection, then dead & buried—was transparently a pretext only. The fact is, besides worrying his son, old Milnes liked to be mentioned as a man who had refused a Peerage.

In this quandary, Dicky, who was himself not incapable of generous feelings & conduct, gave me credit for a similar

* 'His Grace' written above.

constitution & determined to appeal to me. His father, in order probably to vex him always declared, that he was a follower of mine, & could not as a man of honor accept a dignity from my opponents. Dicky threw himself upon my good feelings—& I saw his father & said & urged everything which should induce him to re-consider his course—but in vain. I even ventured to represent to him, that even if the Tories returned to power, & Lord Derby were to consult me as to the commoners who should be promoted—the number must necessarily be limited & would be confined to those members of the House of Commons who had served the party long, made great sacrifices, & left behind them great influences. That private friendship merely could not be a ground of promotion. I thought that this representation of affairs at one moment a little shook him—but he was ultimately firm—& he died a Commoner.

Lady Palmerston always said that the younger Milnes was too ridiculous to make a Peer, & that it could only have been managed by inheritance. Suddenly we were again in office—old Milnes not being then, I think dead—& the family, including Lord Galway, who had every claim on the party, made a strong appeal to me to put the matter right. The title then was to be De Rhodes, & young Milnes engaged that if it were granted, the seat at Pomfret, so far as the Fryston interest was involved, should be secured to the Tories. But it was quite out of the question.

Five years after Dicky was made Lord Houghton—by Lord Pam.

Milnes the father was a tall, handsome man with a distinguished presence. Lord Houghton was unfortunately short, with a face like a Herculaneum masque, or a countenance cut out of an orange. His mouth was a long slit. By self indulgence, he had become when middleaged red & fat. Though affecting the serious, & very mouthy & magniloquent in his speeches which were quite intolerable, his real talent, like his visage, was humorous & comic. He was a capital performer in charades, & generally in the humorous parts of private theatricals. G. Smythe with reference to his appearance, & his fun of which he was ashamed used to call him Sancho Pança.

He told me, that he would sooner be an Under-Secretary of State, than a Peer, but that Palmerston had been prejudiced against him in that light. I ventured to remind him, that had he stuck to his party, he certainly might have been U.S. & probably something much higher. He began to blubber, & say, that he always had a singular affection for me, & looked unutterable love in the highest style of comedy. I put him right by some gossip, & after telling me two or three good stories, he went out of the room splitting with laughter.

[28]

George Smythe used to say 'I don't pretend to have any principle, but I have some heart, & I am a gentleman.'

He had a theory, that characters were always reproduced. Of Milnes he would say 'Bozzy to the life: it explains everything.' (Boswell)

Milnes was 25 years speaking in Parliament & he is the only man of whom it can be said, that, beginning badly, everytime he spoke worse.

He never caught the House of Commons' tone. Too easy & familiar in society, the moment he was on his legs in St Stephen's, he was nervous, took refuge in pomposity, & had no flow; a most elaborate style & always recalling his words. His irresistibly comic face becoming every moment more serious, produced the effect of some celebrated droll, Liston or Keeley, & before he had proceeded five minutes, though he might be descanting on the wrongs of Poland or the rights of Italy, there was sure to be a laugh.

[29]

'Ada' used to shock Lytton by her barefaced atheism. He maintained a correspondence with her on the Immortality of the Soul, which will probably some day be published, for he never wrote an invitation to dinner without an eye to posterity.

At one time, he flattered himself, that he had a little shaken her; she had hinted at some sort of Pantheistic compromise. 'Never' said Lytton 'I *must* have *identity*.'

He wanted to be a popular author, a distinguished orator, & a Baronet in the Kingdom of Heaven—with Knebworth Park to boot! He very truly said to me on a memorable occasion, when he wanted me to make him a Peer, & I wished to make him a Secretary of State 'Remember this my dear friend; I speak to you solemnly; you are dealing now with the vainest man that perhaps ever existed.'

He exceeded Cicero.

[30]

Bulwer said to me one day, in his sort of confidential, pompous, style—perhaps, instead of pompous, I should rather say oracular 'One of the advantages of public life is that it renews Youth. A Cabinet Minister at fifty may not absolutely be a young man, but he is a young Cabinet Minister.'

Youth was the master-feeling of Bulwer. H. Baillie said, when the world was discussing why Bulwer parted with his wife 'He wants *bonnes fortunes*.' H.B. though known in public life afterwards as a dry, cantankerous body, had heard in his time the chimes o' night. He was supposed to have been a lover of Lady Blessington in Sicily: at any rate, was her friend in London: knew Bulwer early through that house: had lived in the coulisses of the London French Play when it was high fashion, & had kept Jennie Coulon.

Twenty years after H.B. had said this to me at Lady Blessington's in Seamore Place, Bulwer was sitting next to me in the House of Commons a ci-devant Cabinet Minister which I had made him, & watching Palmerston at 70 making a triumphant speech. Palmerston had said nothing, as usual, rich or rare; but there was noise, gaiety, health. Bulwer looked fascinated. 'That man' he whispered to me in his Delphic tones 'is a future.'

The Emperor of the French was a very romantic man.

[31]

When Palmerston made his famous attack on Lord Aberdeen (about 1848 or so) & intimated, that the future Prime Minister under whom he was to serve, was a piece of 'antiquated imbecility', Lord Aberdeen said 'What an impudent fellow! I was at school with him, & he is three months older than I am.'

Lord Aberdeen was at Harrow with Palmerston, & Peel. They all lived to be Premiers.

One of the great impostures of political gossip, which has however served its turn, was the modern myth promoted by the followers of Lord Palmerston, that he was the friend & successor of Canning. Canning personally disliked him, & thought meanly, too meanly, of his abilities. He never would admit him into the Cabinet; though he was hard pressed for men, & was obliged to have recourse to old Sturges Bourne, whom he revived for the occasion.

[32]

Dining in the open air at Gunnersbury—in a summer evening— on the Terrace Lyndhurst there (87 or about) conversation on Canning—Charles Villiers tried to bring out some reminiscences, Lyndhurst having been his Lord Chancellor. After some time, & several interesting details, Lyndhurst asked how old Canning was when he died. Answer 57. '57' Lyndhurst exclaimed—'a mere boy!'

Of founding families Lord Ellenborough said 'there is always a Sybarite in the third generation'.

Just before the Russian war (1853–4) the Duchess Dowager of Somerset plaguing Lord Palmerston with questions—'what will happen?' &c &c—at last he said 'I can't see farther than my nose —& mine is a very short one.'

The King of the Belgians much alarmed at the naval preparations of France (1858 or 9), after a long conference with me said 'We must take care that Rule Britannia does not become an old song.'

Walking up St James's St with Thackeray, passing White's he

said 'There are only two things which an Englishman can't get; the Garter & White's.'

[33]

Macaulay said to Madame de Rothschild who was complaining of persons extolling Louis Napoleon whom she hated, even at the expense of the great Founder, 'No; it is not exactly that; he is different: it is Julius Caesar & Augustus Caesar again.'

Peel said of Henry Drummond's speaking, that 'it was very good for ten minutes'. He could not sustain it.

Lytton who was always mourning over his lost youth, & was ridiculously made up, delighted in Palmerston, leading the House of Commons at 76! He sate opposite him with an expression of contemplative admiration. It was not however his wit, or his eloquence, or his dexterity that excited this sentiment. It was his age. 'That man' he said to me one day 'is a future.'

[34]

I was never fortunate in hearing Macaulay to great advantage. I should like to have heard him among men, when he held forth, & was what Sydney Smith called 'A book in breeches'. I remember we met him one day at dinner at Lord Lyveden's, then Vernon Smith—but it was a ladies' party—& I can't conceive under any circumstances his conversation could have adapted itself to female society. There was no grace in it: he could be sarcastic, & witty, but never playful. He talked a good deal this day, but the women thought him pedantic. Generally speaking I should say, he wanted what Lord George Bentinck used to call 'charm'.

[35]

I dined at Comte Molé's (I think 1842) & sate next to Alexander Humboldt at dinner. He was then a very old man, though he lived ten years more. But he had none of the infirmities of age: being

vivacious, & both communicative & sympathising. I am ashamed
to recall so little, when the effect was so pleasing. Victor Hugo
sate opposite to me; a handsome man, not then more than forty,
& looking younger.

MaryAnne used to say 'Manners change even more, than features.'

Smythe used to say 'Bulwer is dying of Dickens—& yet can't be
without him. The moth & the candle. Just come up from Knebworth, Dickens & Co. acting in the Hall. Bulwer to give a piece
of land to build cottages (retreats) for scribblers. Fancies it marks
the difference between his position & Dickens'—& dying all the
time of jealousy & envy combined.'

1862

The Prince Napoleon visited England—was at the Clarendon
Hotel: left his card personally at Grosvenor Gate. I was obliged,
therefore, to ask for an audience, though I had wished not to
have met him at this time. His resemblance to the portraits of the
first Emperor complete: &, so far as I can judge from what I have
heard & read, the resemblance equally striking in manner.
Immensely clever; extraordinary conversational eloquence; fiery
vivacity; pantomime gesture.

The object of his conversation, which lasted an hour, was to
impress upon me the importance to both countries of a frank
understanding between the Tories & his family. 'You all say you
are for the French alliance—but the French alliance means surely
something for France. We are ready to act with England in every
way, but the moment we seek to derive anything from the alliance,
which justifies it to our country, & reconciles them to it, then
there is a general outcry. Is this reasonable? Is it possible to go
on in this way? Is France to feel that the alliance is merely a
complimentary phrase? We supported you in the Russian* war,
which was clearly an English interest: in China where we have
nothing to do; we are always ready to act with you—& for British
interests—to waive points not absolutely exigent, for your con-
venience. Are our interests not to be considered also? It is not
possible for the Buonapartes to sit still in the slippers of the
Bourbons.'

* 'Crimean' written above.

He thought then the Tories were coming in again—& asked me 'Why do you not take the Foreign Office?'

I replied it was inconsistent with the post of leader of the House of Commons. The united labor was impossible.

In 1856–7, (Dec. Jany.) at the Tuileries, the Emperor said to me 'I have always thought, that the principle of the Anglo-French alliance was this: that France should assist England in her policy —& the converse; but Lord Palmerston seems always to think, that the first condition of the Alliance should alone prevail.' When I left the Tuileries that day—farewell audience, the Emperor having entered into every point, & I having re-iterated my opinion previously expressed, that the then English government would not stand (Lord Palmerston's first government, which was placed in a minority, a few weeks after, shortly after the meeting of Parliament dissolved it, obtained a triumphant majority, & yet were turned out by their own Parliament the succeeding year) I saw the Emperor was quite sceptical as to my opinion & was entirely with Palmerston. His Majesty said to me 'Lord Derby has no men.'

In this same year, 56–7, Prince Napoleon had given me a grand banquet at the Palais Royal. He had asked all the distinguished men of his clientele. Lord Holland & myself the only Englishmen & sate on his right & left hand. Among others I recall, was Chevalier whose brow, though high, seemed to me singularly & suspiciously narrow: E. Girardin, Alfred de Vigny & young Dumas all three of whom I had known in 1842, & all wonderfully changed. Girardin who in old days had coal black hair, cut in a straight line over his severe & sinister brow, & who emulated the *air Napoleon*: with some resemblance: a hideous Buonaparte, had become a white headed man with large green goggle-eyed spectacles, a hideous guignol. Alfred de Vigny, who was supposed to be the prettiest poet not only in his verse but in person in Paris; a slender waist, long auburn locks shading his blooming & ingenuous cheek, & in dress picturesquely dandified, was a corpulent, grey headed oldish gentleman. His original image being stamped on my brain, having myself a memory which never dims, the effect was most remarkable—& I have often experienced it in other cases. Meeting people after an interval of twenty years, it is like people going out of one door of a room in youth, & returning, immediately after through another as old men. I have seen such effects in some plays where there is an interval of a generation between the acts. One naturally immediately asks & feels 'Am I so altered?' I don't think so. Certainly not in feeling.

Well then for young Dumas. This reminds me, that in 1842 I met one evening at the Opera one Charles Le Dru whose acquaintance I had made at Lady Blessington's—an advocate—& great democrat, but very much addicted to the English, a lively, cordial man. He was with my banker John Drummond, & he told me that a provincial poet, of whom much was expected, was to read a tragedy that night after, or before, or at, a supper which he was to give in a sort of barn, or colossal garret, or gigantic artist's studio, quite unfurnished, which was lent him for the occasion—& so I went. And it was a wonderful scene. John & Harvey Drummond & I think George Smythe, & then all the literary heros of whom we had heard so much, Sue & Souliés, Balzac, & many more. I dare say forty persons—rough fare, but plenty—& a host who made everything delightful from his fire & warmth. I sate between John Drummond, & a tall Mulatto, the most animated & excitable being I had ever met. This was Alexander Dumas, who was then a notoriety—hardly a celebrity: he had not written the Mousquetaires & Monte Cristo. He had taken the liberty of bringing without an invitation, his son: a youth of seventeen, extremely slender & fair; a very delicate & interesting lad. This was afterwards the famous Alex. Dumas fils—the hero of the Dame aux Camelias, & the guest of Prince Napoleon on the day I mention. He was a very handsome man, rather above the middle height—fair—but inclining a little too much to embonpoint. I was standing by the Prince before dinner, & every guest was presented to me, & I tried to say something to everyone. I was tolerably successful. I reminded Dumas of our first acquaintance & the scene, which from the after-fate of the poet of the night, might be remembered by any one with interest—but he did not seem to care to recall our literary orgy in the good Le Dru's garret. He had become quite a vrai gentleman—of distinguished bonnes fortunes, & the pulcher Apollo of the demimonde. Now the poet of the garret was Monsieur Ponsard, & the tragedy he read was *Lucrece*, which had an immense success. He even got, I believe, in the Academy; & became better known still in England by a criticism on Shakespeare—whom he described as 'the divine Williams'; an expression which was remembered when the immortal *Lucrece* was forgotten.

The Emperor of the French was a very romantic man. The Queen of England had a great personal influence over him. Unfortunately, the Prince Consort hated him. He said to me once 'He is always a Conspirator: it is the key-note of everything.'

When the Italian war seemed to be inevitable, brought about by the intrigues of Cavour with the Emperor, & when there were secret understandings it was supposed between the parties &c, as a last resource to maintain the peace of Europe, the Queen was advised to avail herself of her presumed personal influence with the Emperor & write to him a private letter. I did not see this letter, though I have no doubt it was well conceived & well expressed: with the advantage of Lord Derby's advice & criticism: but I was permitted to see the Emperor's reply which was only shown to Lord Derby, Lord Malmesbury, & myself. To me it was one of the most interesting & most satisfactory communications under the circumstances possible. Full, & frank. It told everything: how Cavour came, what he said, what was said to him, what was contemplated. It assumed, that all must agree, that the position of Italy was most unsatisfactory to all, & reminded the Queen that at the conferences of Paris, the Emperor had wished to anticipate what seemed to him inevitable by joint action. But whatever the state of Italy, whatever the necessity of acting on the part of France, whatever the conversations & contemplated conduct with Sardinia &c &c, such was his value for the friendship & esteem of 'ma très chère soeur' that he pledged himself, & in language the most solemn, affectionate & precise that notwithstanding all that had passed—he would never attack Austria unless she previously attacked Piedmont.

With this card in our hand, peace seemed secure, & with this Lord Cowley went to Vienna. Who could believe that after this Austria should have attacked Piedmont without any intimation to England, & having attacked her & released the Emperor of the French from his personal pledge, should have behaved with such military imbecility, that for a long time nobody actually knew where the Austrian army were. They crossed & recrossed the frontier, ravaged some of the enemy's land & then retired; & then wandered about like idiots. Nothing could have justified their conduct, but a direct march to Turin. When Lord Cowley went to the Emperor on the news of the invasion of Piedmont arriving, Prince Napoleon was coming out of the royal cabinet—his face radiant!

The young Emperor of Austria was very conceited. He was literally sick of hearing the praises of the Emperor of the French. He had a fine army & longed to command it, for which he had no quality. He said to Lord Cowley 'I know that the French artillery may be superior to mine—but in no other branch have they any pre-eminence.'

In one of the long, frequent, & troubled, interviews which took place between the Emperor & the English Ambassador before the war broke out, the Emperor suddenly turned round & said 'Cannot France & England understand each other?' & hinted at partition. But Lord Cowley would not listen to it. He even went on that, or on a preceding [occasion]—but, I think, on the present one to tell the Emperor that his policy would revive the Northern Alliance against him.

My own opinion is, that, even if Lord Cowley had been our Ambassador at Vienna: certainly if Lord Stratford, or Sir Henry Bulwer had been there, there would have been no war. There wanted the unceasing vigilance of a commanding character to baffle the intrigues of a miserable Camarilla. Our Ambassador, Lord——* Loftus was not fit to be resident at a third rate German Court—& was quite despised & disregarded by that of Vienna. He was a pompous nincompoop—& of all Lord Malmesbury's appointments the worst—& that's saying a good deal.

In defence of Malmesbury, it should be said Lord Stanhope had refused the post—& Malmy. always said he was driven in that & other instances to the office list—but the first quality of a Minister is to select competent instruments, &, I suspect, that Malmy. himself was the tool of his Private Secretary Bidwell—an F.O. man, a jobber, & the employed agent of the man whom he counselled his patron to promote.

* Disraeli's line.

V

ROYAL RECOGNITION

[36]

'J'étais né penseur' Metternich once said to me (1848). Sitting next to a young German Prince, of great intelligence, at dinner at Windsor (I think Prince Victor of Hohenlohe) & mentioning this he pointed to the Prince Consort, to whom he sate next, the ladies having retired, & murmured 'Et lui aussi—né penseur.'

[37]

1859

The Prince Consort, on more than one occasion this year spoke of the Italians to me, as 'a worn out race'.

It is to be noted, that up to this time (1863) they have not produced a man capable of affairs, since Cavour.

The Prince said, that the French required to be 'licked' (his very phrase) once every fifty years: or there was no security for peace & civilisation. The French, he said, were vain, fond of military glory, & fond of pillage. He said they were a little race & always beat in the long run.

The Prince said to me one day, about a year before his death 'Lord John Russell is very fond of quoting King William 3rd & his assertion of our liberties & all that, on which there are two opinions. Why does he not praise William 3 for what he was incontestably illustrious & the merit of which none can contend; viz that he placed himself at the head of a great League against France, & preserved the liberties of Europe.'

1860

I should not be surprised if the great body of writers of fiction, that have flourished in France during the last $\frac{1}{4}$ of a century will ultimately take in their literature the same position as is occupied in ours by the Elizabethan Dramatists.

Among these French writers, two names will, I apprehend, stand out pre-eminent, though their style is very different. I will not speak of George Sand as of Shakespeare, for they have little resemblance, though Balzac may be pitted with Ben Jonson—but Sand is in my opinion, without doubt, the finest prose writer in any modern language—at least. As passionate as Rousseau, & far more picturesque. No writer perhaps ever possessed so fine an eye for nature or could convey the results with such picturesque precision. Dumas, & the others, would be the Marlowes, Massingers, Beaumont & Fletchers, Fords &c.

It will, generally, be found, that all great political questions end in the tenure of Land. What is the nature of that tenure is the first question a Statesman should ask himself, when forming an opinion on public events.

[38]

1863

They were talking about Pitt—someone doubted his powers—had no faith in the theory of heaven-born ministers—a man of 22 or 24 must be a man of 22 or 24 &c &c. John Russell (Earl Russell) said 'No: there are some men who mature early, & some late. Mr Pitt matured at *24* & Lord Palmerston at *74.*'

One of the last dinners at Court—I should think 1859—no one there except the Royal family but Duc d'Aumale & myself. After the Queen had retired, I sate next to Prince Consort, Duc d'Aumale on his right. Never heard better conversation. They got on Julius Caesar. Duc d'A very full on him: 'The most complete character of antiquity' &c &c.

'But a very debauched man' said the P. Consort.

[39]

1863

It is said that the Prince of Wales is too much inclined to practical jokes. Something disagreeable happened this winter when he was on a hunting visit (before his marriage) to the Master of the Horse, the Marquess of Aylesbury. This was one of the first visits of the Prince as his own master. It would seem that his host in this case was the victim of the tour—de force or d'artifice. There was immense surprise, some indignation, but no one liked to interfere. Jemmy Macdonald, finding this to be the case, with characteristic sense & courage, having in his time had something to do with the breaking in of another young Prince—went up to H.R.H. & said 'I am sure your Royal Highness will pardon me; but you are only just entering into life. This is a sort of thing which English gentlemen do not like.'

From what Sir Hamilton Seymour told me this year, it would seem to run rather in the family. Little Prince Alfred came up to him one day at Windsor, & said, in a coaxing tone, 'Did you ever see a monkey?' Sir Hamilton had seen many monkeys. '*Will* you let me show you a monkey?' But Sir Hamilton not caring to leave an agreeable society, declined, & continued to decline, notwithstanding the coaxing voice, & little soft hand, that still held his, & would have drawn him away. At last he yielded to the repeated 'Oh! do let me show you a monkey!' And the boy led him out of the room, where Royalty was present, down a corridor, at the end of which was a tall glass, before which the royal urchin landed Sir Hamilton, & then coolly said 'There's a monkey!'

Strange, that these should be the results of such an education & such a parentage. Fancy the Prince Consort & a practical joke. Some few years ago, I think when the Princess Alice married, Lord Palmerston sent me a message by one of his aides-de-camp, to say he should like to have some conversation with me in his room behind the Speaker's chair. These interviews between the two leaders of the House are not unusual, & between Lord Palmerston & myself were not very rare, & tend to the facility & satisfactory despatch of public business.

I remember on this occasion he began with a characteristic joke. Seating himself with some solemnity, & inviting me to follow his example, he said 'Quite a Cabinet'. However what he wished to confer with me about was the provision for the Princess & other matters connected with the Royal family. He told me what the Government proposed & their reasons. He mentioned one part of the arrangement which involved an alternative & was ready to do that which I thought would be most agreeable to my friends & the house generally. I was in favor of his original plan. Then he came to some proposition for some by no means considerable addition to the Queen's income which I can't at this moment recall, or the exact arrangement by which it was to be accomplished. But I remember the reasons he urged in its favor.

The fact, that after a quarter of a Century, the Court had never got into debt—that it had brought up a very numerous family, & exercised a flowing & dignified hospitality. It was the expenditure for the children that pressed the Queen. Their education had been costly. In some instances, from domestic reasons of wisdom, it had been deemed expedient that the young Princes should have separate establishments, rather prematurely. 'The Queen & the Prince' he said 'are anxious that their children should be perfectly educated. Some may think, their system too elaborate. But the other way has been tried in this country. In the last generation, we had a race of uneducated Princes—& a pretty kettle of fish they made of it.'

[40]

1863

I heard at the end of the last, & at the beginning of this, year, more than once, from great personages about the Court, that the Queen had said, & repeated, that 'Mr Disraeli was the only person, who appreciated the Prince'.

When Parliament met too, Her Majesty had occasion to write personally to Lord Derby respecting the Memorial Monument to the Prince, & some necessary steps that might be taken in Parliament thereon, & she mentioned in the letter, that she had no objection to his conferring with Mr. Disraeli 'towards whom she should always entertain feelings of gratitude for the support which he had always given to the Prince' in all his undertakings for the refinement of public taste & the improvement of society—or some words to that effect.

Lord Derby was generous enough to read this passage of H.M.'s letter to me.

In March the Royal Wedding took place. The Prince of Wales was married to the Princess of Denmark at Windsor. This alliance made a great sensation & excitement in the Country. The long-pent up feeling of affectionate devotion to the Queen & of sympathy with her sorrows, came out with that deep & fervid enthusiasm, for which the people of England are, I think, remarkable. But the excitement of the nation with their public receptions, & addresses, & processions, & splendid gifts, & the long vista of universal festivity, which was planned, & which lasted the whole season, was quite equalled among the Aristocracy, as to who should, or rather would, be invited to the Royal Wedding.

As the beautiful Chapel of St George was very limited, & as there were a considerable number of Royal guests, & as the principal persons of the Household, the Ambassadors, the Knights of the Garter, & the Cabinet Ministers—were as a matter of course to be invited, it became an interesting question where the line was to be drawn. At last it was whispered about, that the limit was to be Duchesses. But as time drew on, nobody seemed to be asked, & some great persons received suspicious invitations to a breakfast at Windsor Castle *after* the ceremony. At the same time, tickets began to circulate in influential quarters, permitting the bearers to places in the Cathedral nave, without the chapel, in order to see the processions pass.

At last, however, about a fortnight before the ceremony or less, it was announced, that as there were only ——* seats in the Chapel, & as Sovereigns & Royal Princes, Knights of the Garter & their wives, Cabinet Ministers & ambassadors & great Officers of the Household & their wives would nearly fill it, there were necessarily few seats for H.M.'s private friends.

The disappointment & excitement equally increased. I have heard that when the list was finally submitted to her Majesty, there were only four places not, as it were, officially appropriated. Her Majesty named Lord & Lady De la Warr her earliest friends, & myself & my wife.

There is no language, which can describe the rage, envy, & indignation of the great world. The Duchess of Marlborough went into hysterics of mortification at the sight of my wife, who

* Disraeli's line.

was on terms of considerable intimacy with her, & said it was really shameful after the reception which the Duke had given the Prince of Wales at Blenheim, & as for the Duchess of Manchester, who had been Mistress of the Robes in Lord Derby's Administration, she positively passed me for the season without recognition.

However we went, & nothing could be more brilliant, & effective, than the whole affair was. It is the only pageant which never disappointed me. The beautiful chapel, the glittering dresses, the various processions, 1st the Knights of the Garter, of the Royal personages, of the Bridegroom, of the Bride—the heralds, the announcing trumpets, the suspense before the processions appeared, the magnificent music, the Queen in widowed garments in her Gothic Cabinet—all deeply interesting or effective.

I had never seen the Queen since the catastrophe, & ventured, being nearsighted, to use my glass. I saw H.M. well & unfortunately caught her glance—perhaps she was looking to see whether we were there, & triumphing a little in the decided manner in which she had testified 'her gratitude'. I did not venture to use my glass again.

The Prince of Wales who was habited as a Knight of the Garter deported himself with great dignity, & conducted himself at the Altar where he was left an unusual time alone, from some accident that occurred in the Procession of the Bride, with grace & tact—all eyes being upon him.

The way in which the Royal personages looked up & bowed to the Royal Cabinet was singularly graceful & imposing—& in this respect the Princess Mary of Cambridge exceeded them all. Her demeanour was most dignified.

After the ceremony, the festival was very joyous; a great number of guests who had been invited to the breakfast at the Castle then appearing—I should say 5 or 600 persons. The Royal personages breakfasted apart—but the mistake was made of not inviting the Ambassadors & their wives to this exclusive repast, who took rank above all the Royal guests who were inferior to their Sovereigns whom they personally represented.

Comte Apponyi was wroth on this head, & certainly the Hungarian dress of Madame Apponyi which had only arrived the night before justified any distinction. It was the most gorgeous & graceful costume ever worn—bright blue velvet, richly embroidered in gold, & astounding sables, but the fancy of the dress exceeded its costly materials.

They had lodgings at Windsor, & the ambassadress changed her costume before she left Windsor. This was fortunate, for the arrangements for departure were bad; the ladies were mobbed at the station, & as many of them had tiaras of diamonds, they were in danger of being plundered. Madame Apponyi was separated from the Ambassador; I rescued her, & got her into a railway carriage with my wife & some others—grand dames, who had lost their husbands. I think I had to sit on my wife's lap. When we got to Paddington in the rain, there was no Ambassadorial carriage—but ours was there & so we took home safe this brilliant & delightful person.

A great lady of the Court, who was my secret friend, & proved herself on many occasions a real one, told me at the breakfast, that the Queen meant to see me. She repeated, that the Queen said she was determined to see me. From which & other things, I inferred that there had been difficulties put in the way.

Lord Derby had had an audience of H.M. before the wedding, on the alleged ground of conferring about the Memorial—but understood as a token of H.M.'s return to public life, & that she would commence to see her Ministers socially, & exalted persons who had been near her person. Lord Derby never mentioned any of the details of this audience to me, but his son did. The Queen received him in her closet sitting; the audience was by no means brief, & Lord Derby stood the whole time, although recovering from a severe fit of the gout. The Queen even alluded to this, & said she feared he would suffer by standing, but offered no seat. So severe was the etiquette.

Notwithstanding my private intimation, time rolled on, & I never heard anything of my audience. Weeks, even months, passed. The Queen had received all her principal Ministers, Lord Clarendon & Lord Derby, & there it stopped. I saw my friend occasionally in society, & once she asked me, whether I had heard anything, & when I replied in the negative, she said, 'Be sure, you will, for H.M. said only the other day, she was determined to see Mr D.'

On   I received an invitation to Windsor Castle for & to stay till the next day.*

* The blank spaces are in the manuscript. The invitation was for 22 April 1863.

When I arrived at the Castle, I received a note from Biddulph telling me that the Queen would receive me before dinner, at a ¼ past seven o'clock. He gave me the hint, that I might make my toilette early, & so be able to leave the presence chamber for the banquet, which was about an hour after. After I was dressed, there came another note to say that Lord John Russell had arrived from town with important despatches, & that the Queen would be engaged & would postpone my audience till the morrow after breakfast.

It was the beginning of the Polish Insurrection, & the Ministry were much perplexed. The despatches were about Poland.

I was struck at dinner by the contrast with the somewhat subdued tone that prevailed in former days at the royal dinners.

The Prince & Princess of Wales were our host & hostess. The party large though consisting only of courtiers (there were more than two households blended) the only guests being Earl Russell & myself. The Prince of Wales gave me the idea of a young man who had just come into a large estate & was delighted at entertaining his friends. He took out his sister, the Princess Helena, & sate opposite the Princess of Wales, who was taken out by Prince Alfred. On the other side of Prince Alfred, was the Countess of Desart (in waiting) & I sate between her & Lady Augusta Bruce, sister of Lord Elgin, whom I had met before at Windsor, when she was in attendance on the Duchess of Kent. I was glad to renew my acquaintance with her, for, like all her family, she is clever, & told me in the course of the dinner a great deal.

When the ladies had retired, I was next to Prince Alfred, who invited me to take Lady Desart's vacated seat. I had not seen him since he was a very young & very little Midshipman. Though still in his teens, he was much altered, had grown a great deal, a bronzed & manly countenance, with a thoughtful brow; altogether like his father. His brother, the Prince of Wales was a Guelph, not a Coburg. The Queen said he was exactly like a portrait which they had there of Frederick, Prince of Wales. I thought him very like a portrait also at Windsor of his [great-] grandfather, George the third, shortly after his accession. Lord Malmesbury said, that his general resemblance to his [great-] grandfather was so great, that he already was always asking questions & talking loud.

Prince Alfred had just recovered from a severe, & dangerous

fever, which had prevented [his] being at the wedding. He was detained by it at Malta, & the telegrams which were constant were so alarming, that one day they feared the wedding could not take place. Alluding to his illness & Malta, we naturally talked of his travels—he had seen a great deal, having been at (the Africa Cape) &c.—on all of which he spoke with simplicity & sense. He was glad to be home again. I remember he said 'What a fine Castle this is. I never saw anyone in any country to be compared with it. I love this Castle; I was born in it.'

When we returned to the Saloon, the circle was formed as if the Queen were present, but the Prince & Princess did not make the round. She kept apart, & then the Prince came & addressed Lord Russell in the circle, & then led him to the Princess with whom he conversed for about ten minutes. Then, after a very short space the Prince came to me, & conversed a little. He asked me, whether I thought the Bill for abolishing the City Police would pass? I replied, that I had not given any personal attention to the subject, but my impression was not favorable to its success. He said he had heard the same, but it ought to pass; there ought to be only one police for the Capital. I perceived from this what I afterwards had proof of, that the passing of the Bill was a capital point with the Court. The opposition to the Bill turned out to be so general throughout the country, that it was eventually withdrawn by the Ministry without a division; not before however several courtiers, who had seats in the House of Commons, making speeches against it, made the discomfiture more flagrant, as well as the particular animus more obvious.

After this, the Prince proposed that he should present me to H.R.H. & I went up accordingly. I had, therefore, at last, a good opportunity of forming an opinion of her appearance; which was highly favorable. Her face was delicate & refined; her features regular; her brow well-moulded; her mouth beautiful; her hair good & her ears small. She was very thin. She had the accomplishment of being gracious without smiling. She had repose. She spoke English, but not with the fluency I had expected, & I don't think she always comprehended what was said. The Prince hovered about her, & after a few minutes joined the conversation.

I remember nothing very particular about it except that it fell upon nightingales, & I asked H.R.H. whether she knew what nightingales fed upon. While she was confessing her ignorance &

her curiosity the Prince came & she addressed the question to him, which he could not answer. I told them—upon glowworms; exactly the food which nightingales should require. The Prince was interested by this & exclaimed 'Is that a fact, or is it a myth?'

'Quite a fact, Sir; for my woodman is my authority, for we have a great many nightingales at Hughenden, & a great many glowworms.'

'We have got one nightingale at Sandringham' said the Prince smiling.

I remember now, that the conversation got to nightingales in this manner. The Princess told me that they were delighted with their London residence. They awoke in the morning, & looked into a garden, & heard the birds sing. I said then 'I fear not nightingales, Madam.'

After this, there was the private band, just the same as if H.M. were present—& at 11 o'clock the Prince & Princess & attendants retired.

On the morrow I breakfasted with the Lady in waiting & the maids of Honor, & Lord John Russell. We had a merry breakfast, for the ladies wished to make Lord John & myself talk—& I, who was really somewhat nervous from my approaching interview, was glad to take refuge in raillery. Lord John was genial, which, on the whole, he generally has been with me. For notwithstanding our fierce public struggles for long years, & the crusade I have always preached against High Whiggism, of which he was the Incarnate creation, there were really some elements of sympathy between us, being with all his hauteur & frigid manner, really a man of sentiment, & imagination, & culture.

When breakfast was over, we were left together, & I asked him seriously what was the real state of affairs in Poland. He spoke with great frankness on the matter, & among other things, that the Cabinet had sent a secret agent to Poland in order to obtain some accurate information (I think, Oliphant) 'but I can't say' he added 'we are much the wiser. The best opinions seem to hold, that it will be put down in the summer—but' & he shrugged his shoulders 'it may not be—& then——'.

He went to town—& I was left alone with the newspapers. In about a quarter of an hour I was summoned. The attendant led me down part of the great Gallery, & then turned off into a familiar corridor, & then through an antechamber, I was ushered into Prince Albert's special room: a small cabinet, decorated with all the objects of art he loved, & in which I had frequently had the privilege of conferring, & listening at length to his views on public life & politics; when throwing off his reserve & shyness, he warmed into eloquence, not unmixed with sarcastic humor, but on all subjects on which he spoke, distinguished by his perfect knowledge & his thought. The room was quite unchanged. It was in every respect as if he had resided in it yesterday—the writing materials, the books, all the indications of habitual occupation. Only one change I observed: a plate on his accustomed chair—with an inscription 'This was the Prince Consort's chair from 18— to 1861'.

In less than five minutes from my entry, an opposite door opened, & the Queen appeared.

She was still in Widow's mourning, & seemed stouter than when I last saw her, but this was perhaps only from her dress. I bowed deeply when she entered, & raised my head with unusual slowness, that I might have a moment for recovery. Her countenance was grave, but serene & kind—& she said, in a most musical voice, 'It is some time since we met.'

Then to some murmuring words of mine H.M. said 'You have not had a very busy session this year?' In assenting to this, I expressed my wish, that politics were in general as serene as the House of Commons. Upon this H.M. entered into the state of public affairs with frankness & some animation, which entirely removed the first embarrassment of the audience. It was then like an audience between a Sovereign & a Minister.

H.M. expressed her conviction, that whatever happened, the American Union could not be restored. She spoke fully about Poland, nor was it difficult to recognise that the insurrection alarmed her from its possible consequences, on the state of Germany. H.M., however, was quite clear, was sanguine that the Russians would suppress it by the Summer.

She asked me, frankly, whether I thought the present Ministry would get through the Session. I said they were weak, but there was no desire to displace them unless a stronger one could be established. She said she hoped no crisis would be brought about wantonly, for in her forlorn condition, she hardly knew what she could do. I said H.M.'s comfort was an element in all our considerations, & that no action would be taken, I felt sure, unless from commanding necessity.

She said 'Lord Palmerston was grown very old.'

I replied 'But his voice in debate, Madam, is as loud as ever.'

'Yes!' she exclaimed with animation 'and his handwriting!— Did you ever see such a handwriting! So very clear & strong! Nevertheless, I see in him a great change, a very great change. His countenance is so changed.'

Then H.M. turning from public affairs, deigned to say, that it had given her great pleasure to observe, that I had been chosen trustee of the British Museum in the place of the late Lord Lansdowne—& she spoke for some time on kindred subjects, alluding to what the Prince had done rather than directly referring to him herself.

At last she asked after my wife & hoped she was well, & then with a graceful bow, vanished.

VI

OBSERVATIONS ON LIFE AND LETTERS

[41]

When Du Chaillu's book came out, & the world was mad about monkeys, several were sceptical as to the Gorillas—but Gladstone said that was the only part of his book of which he felt confident, as he had sate in the House of Commons with a Gorilla for several years—G.P. Bentinck (M.P. for Norfolk). G.P. Bentinck was upwards of 6 feet 2 i. at least, with bandy legs, & the most in-human face ever encountered. It really was a caricature of a Gorilla.

Fred. Lygon, who was the best-looking fellow in the House, said, that he thought Gladstone, as usual, was unfair, & that Bentinck was rather 'the missing link'.

Lord Shelburne used to say that perfect society were wives without husbands & husbands without wives.

Old Lady Cork used to say 'My dear, if you want a dinner party to go off well, don't have two of the same name.'

[42]

Sidney Herbert could not ring his R*s*. Granville Vernon (one of the sons of the Archbishop of York, & brother of Vernon Harcourt, the M.P. for Oxfordshire, & husband of Lady Walde-grave) who was considered the greatest bore in the House & per-haps in society, but who was a man of great information & good ability & had been in the House of Commons all his life when Dr Lushington had made a most eloquent speech, with great knowl-edge of the subject, but which produced little effect, on my expressing some surprise thereat, said to me 'I have observed no man in this house can have great success, who can't sound his R*s*.'

87

It was a melancholy day for human nature when that stupid Lord Anson, after beating about for three years, found himself again at Greenwich. The circumnavigation of our globe was accomplished, but the illimitable was annihilated & a fatal blow [dealt] to all imagination.

Though I always hated breakfasting out, I could not one day decline a proposal from the American Minister, Everett; he was so amiable & polished a man. I think it must have been about 44 or 45. I had published something very successful, *Coningsby* or *Sybil.* He lived in Grosvenor Place. I found there Bunsen, some great Diplomatist, who has gone out of my memory, Macaulay, then in the House of Commons, Dean Milman, Whewell the Master of Trinity. It should have been an agreeable breakfast, if such things can be in England, where men are generally distrait with the impending business of the day. Our host kind & popular, his wife agreeable, his daughter pretty, & buttering delightful cakes of maize for us in American style—& wondrous men. But Bunsen, whom I saw for the first time & whose appearance was not fascinating, took the whole parole to himself. I am always content to be an audience, but I should like to have listened to Macaulay.

Bunsen, short, very stout, with a florid German face, high forehead, blueyed & perspiring, speaking at the pitch of a voice of unparalleled dissonance, never ceased for a moment, even with his mouth full, shrieking his harsh English. All I remember of this memorable breakfast was his screaming out 'Modern History commences with Abraham.'

George Smythe used to say of Bunsen 'That Usher!'

[43]

When they spoke to Sir Robert Peel of some promising speaker out of the House, & who ought to be got into Parliament, he would say 'Can he reply?'

Louis Philippe said one night 'What is the use of conquest? Vassalage is impossible in this age. What is a King? Chief Magistrate, Chief Magistrate.'

Lytton would say when talking of a subject, on which he was pressed to speak 'I have not got the backbone of the speech.'

'Canning had no flow' said Lord Ellesmere, formerly Francis Egerton, his friend & favorite. 'At a dinner party with a few friends, he would talk but it was always raillery. He liked a butt.'

Canning never looked you in the face.

'I have always considered "l'Autriche comme le vrai type d'une Empire"' Metternich said to me.

Somebody said to Peel when Croker was making a considerable speech on the Reform Bill of 1832, that personally Croker was like Canning. Peel a little started, & looking round with his sly, grave, face said 'Mr Canning was a very good looking man!'

Charles Buller said of the 'great Rebellion'—speaking of it as perhaps the greatest event of modern history—'it was the last time a nation believed'.

Philosophically considered, it might be looked upon as the influence of Hebrew Literature on the northern mind—as no doubt the translator of the Bible did it all.

Sir H. Bulwer said of Lord Clarendon (1864) he was a high stepping horse, but made no progress. Reminds me of what Osborne said of Spencer Walpole. He was 'a prancing hearse horse'.

Bulwer said to me: (we were talking of destinies, modes of life &c) 'yours is clear; you will die in harness'.

After giving any account to Lord Ponsonby of any interview with a *personage*, he would say 'Did he caress you?'

[44]

1861

Speaking of the ancients, Lord John Russell said to me 'They had a peculiar talent of saying great things.'

1862

Sir Francis Burdett said to Lord Stratford de Redcliffe (Stratford Canning) on the death of his eminent kinsman 'It was fortunate for his fame (George Canning) that he died. He would not have been equal to the rough task impending.'

Lord S de R. thought, on the contrary, there was great developement going on in the case of G.C.—but spoke hesitatingly.

Lord John Russell wrote to me, apropos of my life of George Bentinck, that George Canning was unfortunate in his biographer, for Stapleton wrote an unreadable life of a brilliant man.

Lord George Bentinck was Canning's private Secretary, who was his uncle by marriage.

G. Smythe (Lord Strangford) said to me, many years ago, that in the three great occasions of his life—Burke was wrong: America: India: France.

In 1856 after the breakup of Lord Aberdeen's Government, Lord John Russell & Lord Derby, who both made great mistakes in the course they took; the latter almost a ruinous one; both said & acted on the belief, that 'Lord Palmerston could not form a government'. Yet Lord Russell & Lord Derby were two of the most experienced men in our public life then existing.

1862

My visit to Lyndhurst after 90 & recovering from a considerable illness; quite unchanged—easy as $\frac{1}{2}$ a century before.

1862

Lord Derby's (not then in office) first audience of the Queen after the death of the Prince Consort—some months?

The Queen talked freely of the Prince: he *would* die: he seemed not to care to live. Then she used these words 'He died from want of what they call pluck.'

Lord Derby not then minister—but was Chairman of the Memorial to the Prince or something. There was an excuse to see him.

Sir Anthony Rothschild—the most good-natured & goodtempered fellow I ever knew—used to say 'Something always happens to vex one.'

[45]

1860

John Russell told me a story of something, which, I think, happened in his travels—but I'm not sure about that. There came a conjuror or magician to a village, & he was ready to tell anything. There were a great many women at the Inn; mostly young, & they were the most curious. But the magician required the hand of a Pucelle before he could read their fates. A check—some consternation. They all hurried out of the room—immense consultation. At last after a great deal of giggling behind the door it opened & they pushed in a child of ten years old, calling out 'Voici la Pucelle'.

1862

Called on Lyndhurst & talked much with him.

I told him that in Devonshire, from which I had just come I had employed myself in reading after many years critically περι στεφανου.* He was quite eager. 'Well, speak the truth? What did you think of it?' And then, much to my surprise, for his taste was austere, he depreciated Demosthenes & placed Cicero far above him. He thought the personal abuse in Demosthenes insufferable—no invention, no taste: mere scolding. Put the Pro Milone et pro Corona together! No comparison—the last a masterpiece, a treasury of oratoric power & skill.

Lord Mendip (old Welbore Ellis) told my father, that he sate in all the Parliaments of Sir Robert Walpole, & he never remembered a speech exceeding half an hour.

I happened to mention this to the Speaker (sitting next to him at dinner) (Evelyn Denison) who doubted, & made researches, & after some days called me to him in the House to show me their result. He produced with triumph a speech of elder Pitt—an hour

* *On the Crown*, by Demosthenes.

& forty minutes. I knew all about that, for it is mentioned in H. Walpole's memoirs—but this would not do. It was after Sir Robert's fall.

Pitt began to introduce long speeches—but for a long time House of Commons was mere declamation. A little commerce & finance sometimes which nobody understood except Sir Robert, & Sir John Barnard—& he was not long.

The Walpoles were a very strange family. Lord Walpole's (present Lord Orford) character drawn prophetically by Horace W. in one of his letters. Lady Dorothy Nevill, his sister, a very clever woman: equal to Professor Hooker as a botanist, without [doubt] the finest pinetum & conservatories & collections of rare trees in the world—all formed & collected & created by herself at Dangstein—introduced the silk worm into England fed on Acanthya or something—& wrote a very good pamphlet in advocacy—the finest & most fanciful emblazoner in the world— & without absolute beauty, wild & bewitching, & yet she never had read one of Horace Walpole's letters, or indeed anything else except the 'Morning Post'.

[46]

1862

The Bishop of Oxford said of dreams, that when you think you recollect them, all that you recollect is the last incident, the crowning incident. He dilated on this, as if it were a Scientific axiom. I doubted it at the time, & have since observed accordingly. My experience does not justify the opinion of the Bishop of Oxford.

Bishop of Oxford said his average correspondence (*letters he received*) was nearly 100 per week. This exceeds the average of a Minister of State with a great Department, or that of the Leader of the House of Commons in the Session.

1848

Guizot said to me 'If the King had retired to St. Cloud, & summoned the Chambers there, he would have surmounted all his difficulties.'

Lord Derby was very punctilious in his pronunciation of English, though his son talked a Lancashire patois. Lord Derby would insolently correct Lord Granville across the House of Lords. Lord Granville always said 'wropped up'—'wrapped' Lord Derby would say in a tone clear to the Reporters. As he would sometimes say to me 'If we look to what Lord Granville calls the "arithmetic" of the question.'

Gladstone was provincial, but a very fine voice. Peel always 'pūt' a question, & to the last said 'woonderful' & 'woonderfully'. He guarded his aspirates with immense care. I have known him trip. The correctness was not spontaneous. He had managed his elocution like his temper: neither was originally good.

[47]

1862

Lady Emma Talbot, daughter of Lord Derby, going down to breakfast this year, on her birth-day, found a checque from her father in her napkin for £5,000 (five thousand). They had been greatly mortified by the alliance. Colonel Talbot having been Lord Derby's private Secretary. But though a younger son, his family was not inferior to that of the Stanleys, being a Talbot & the brother of the Earl of Shrewsbury.

[48]

1862

This year on Lady Emma Talbot's birth-day, coming down to breakfast, she found a birth-day present in her napkin—a checque from Lord Derby for £5000 (five thousand pounds)——

1852

Shortly after the formation of this government, Baron Brunnow, the Russian Ambassador, proposed to Lord Derby an alliance between England & Russia, offensive & defensive. Lord Derby at once rejected the proposition. It was never brought before the Cabinet. But it was made. It should be remembered the position of France was then very menacing; the French Empire was nearly hatched. We had good information as to Louis Napoleon's (then President of the Republic for ten years) intentions on this head. A month before the imperial declaration, a drawing of Louis Napoleon in full imperial robes & paraphernalia, was entrusted to a Lithographic artist with positive instructions to take off only one impression. One, however, was sent to me, by a secret agent. I possess it now.

Walking with Thiers in the Champs Elysées, one morning (1845–6 perhaps: it might have been 1842–3) Madame Lieven passed us, alone. Thiers saluted her with high consideration, & naturally spoke of her the moment she was out of hearing. He seemed to rate her very highly, & referring to the former social splendor of her life; Ambassadress at great courts &c &c; & her present very reduced position, he said it made no difference, observing 'Les grands personnages ne sont jamais médiocres.'

Guizot, who passed his days with Madame Lieven, always quitted her an hour before her salon commenced, & when he returned to attend it, always addressed her, as if he had not seen her since the previous evening.

On the whole, I prefer the perfume of fruit even to that of flowers. It is more mystical & thrilling; more rapturous.

Stanley said to me, (about 1856) 'I am not much of a prophet, but there is one thing, I think, I do foresee in this country—& that is a great Ecclesiastical crash.'

1863

Baroness Lionel de Rothschild told me, that Gladstone was writing a history of Porcelain, & that he frequently was with Mr Barker in Piccadilly, the most learned authority on such matters, examining his rare collections & specimens, & availing himself of Barker's unrivalled taste & information.

Mem. I was in Paris—winter of 1842–3
                              of 1845–6
                              of 1856–7

Lord Lyndhurst had been reading a great deal upon races with much interest. 'Nothing' he said 'will induce me to believe that the human species could have sprung from one pair.' This was about 1853 or 4. At present, he is ten years older, to my mind in the same command of intellect as ever—but they say that Lady Lyndhurst, who persecutes him on the subject, has a religious gentleman, of very low views, constantly with him, & I observe on his table, volumes of the Prophecies, & all that. For though he is 91, he can read the 'Times' everyday—his great delight. Lady Lyndhurst seems satisfied with his spiritual condition, & I am told he listens with much edification to the Gentleman. The truth is Lord Lyndhurst now loves nothing so much as conversation, & he must have somebody to talk to him, no matter what the subject.

[49]

George Smythe said, that, as they say, novelists always draw their own characters, he wished to God Thackeray would draw his own —that would be a character! The Cynic Parasite!

The Duke of Beaufort (late Duke; 1863) used to say, that Town life was favorable to a youthful appearance. That people who always lived in the country got to look older so much sooner than the habitués of London. He attributed this to selfishness, self indulgence & not living with the desire to please. People, always in the country, got grey & red & stout & coarse—& stooped & poked. I think myself that age, to a certain degree, is a habit.

But of course much depends on constitution. Lady Jersey is as vivacious, as versatile & volatile, at 78—seventy eight (which she must now be; 1863) as in her youth. No one could associate her with the idea of age. Nor does she look like an old woman. Her eyes are flashing, her lips red, her shoulders once famous, still round & white, her hair very good, though somewhat grey, which she does not attempt to disguise—she never makes up in the least. No white paint, no rouge, no dyes, no messes & mixtures à l'Imperatrice—but like her conversation, still the child of nature —the spoilt child of nature & society.

Lady Palmerston, her contemporary, is also a marvellous

woman. Immense strength; & energy. But she has not the vivid-
ness of Lady Jersey, & she paints like a sepulchre. I have heard
that Lady Palmerston was older than her Lord.

Lord Lyndhurst's voice at 91 is tremulous, but his conversation
is as good, I would say as youthful, as ever; it was always a mixture of playfulness & sound sense. No one more weighty when
serious, but shrinking from arguments in conversation—& with
the art of apparently touching lightly on subjects, though really
with force.

The most remarkable old man, that I ever knew was the Duc
Pasquier—though latterly he got very deaf. When we were last at
Paris (1856–7), he called on Mrs Disraeli, who was living in an
Hotel of the Rue Rivoli *seconde*—& came up the whole flight of
stairs, dressed in the highest fashion, with boots worthy of
D'Orsay—& most agreeable conversation. He was then past 90.

[50]

When my father published the 2nd part of *Curiosities of Literature*
Palgrave (afterwards Sir Francis) said 'It was the greatest Belles
Lettres book of this age'—but thought the age of Belles Lettres
was past.

Charles Buller looked upon our Puritanic Revolution as perhaps
the most remarkable of modern events. He said 'It was the last
time a nation believed.'

Dining at Bellamy's saying it was a great privilege to live in this
age—electric telegraph, railroads, gold regions &c. &c. Stanley
seemed inclined to deny, that it was peculiarly progressive, &
therefore peculiarly exciting. Said invention of Printing, Mariner's
compass, discovery of America,* quite as great, as anything in our
times. Perhaps mail-coaches produced as great relative effect as
railroads. Said everybody at everytime thought the age critical.
What more critical than the thirty years' war, the ambition of
Louis 14, the American, & the French revolutions? Even in our

---

* Disraeli later inserted 'French Revolution' above, then crossed these
words out.

own time from introduction of the Reform Bill, always great events—supposed critical. The Reform of Parliament itself, the Irish agitation, two French Revolutions, the Crimean War, the Indian Mutiny, the Italian Revolution—& so on.

When Sir Robert Peel died, Bulwer said 'He died because there was nothing more left for him to do.'

[51]

Popular quotations generally wrong. Even Hallam in the preface to his *Constitutional History* quotes 'The monstrous faith of many for one'.

Pope wrote 'the *enormous* faith': much more philosophic & much more poetical. 'Monstrous' mere exclamation of foolish wonder; like Dominie Sampson's 'prodigious!'

There again, there is another line of Pope's in constant use
'A youth of folly, an old age of cards'.
What does this mean? Does Pope mean to contrast cards with folly, so that we may infer cards are wisdom?
He really wrote
'A Youth of *frolics*, an old age of cards'.
By which he admirably contrasted the active folly of youth with the inert folly of age—& combined both gradations in his character.

We constantly read 'caviare to the Multitude'. It is 'caviare to the General'.

By the bye, Shakespeare mentions 'caviare', & Ben Jonson 'botargo'.

Some poets who would be quite forgotten live, & live vigorously, by a single line.

'Fine by degrees, & beautifully less' is a memorable instance.

An often quoted line, & assumed to be classic about Scylla & Charybdis is from a monkish writer.

'The child of misery, baptised in tears' is a fine line & still quoted. From a most, & deservedly, obscure writer; Langhorne.

There used to be well understood rules in the House of Commons in old days (before the Reform) respecting quotations.

No English poet to be quoted, who had not completed his Century.

Greek & French never under any circumstances: Latin as you liked: Horace & Virgil by preference; then Juvenal.

Now quotation (in House of Commons) is what we are most deficient in. Very few will venture on Latin. But it is not that the House has relinquished quotation, but the new elements find their illustrations & exponents in illegitimate means. It is not merely, that they quote Byron & Tennyson before they have completed their quarantine. But Bright & Cobden, & all those sort of people, are always quoting Dickens & *Punch* &c. Our quotations are either tawdry or trashy. The privilege of quotation should not be too easy. It should be fenced in.

When I took the lead of the Opposition, I temperately & discreetly, somewhat revived the habit of classic quotation. (I had done it before to some degree, when I had got the ear of the House.) Applied with discretion, it was not unsuccessful; & I was rather amused in course of time to find Lord John Russell, who was then Prime-Minister & Leader of the House, brushing up his classical reminiscences, & coming down frequently with Virgilian passages, so that he might keep up the credit of his party. If it were worth while to examine *Hansard* for such trifles, this would be found to be accurate.

[52]

G.S.S. did not consider images drawn from natural objects permissible in prose composition—& in poetry to be used with great reserve. Their facility fatal.

Macaulay would never permit the use of the word *'artistic'*— which he deemed a barbarism.

Two interesting traits in Roman life. The introduction of Horace to Maecenas by Virgil—which seemed at first a failure. M. asked him to dinner several months afterwards:

the other that Cleopatra was on a visit to Julius Caesar, at the time of his assassination.

What we want is a more accurate conception of what 'publishing' was among the ancients. From many passages it would seem, that a book was as well known as since the discovery of printing. The 'Pro Milone' was published, not written. It was urged in vindication of Procopius, that his 'Secret History' unlike his other works, was not published. The theme is worthy of a German Scholar: & might have been treated in the old days by Joseph Scaliger or even Salmasius.

Stanley said he could never understand what was meant by Thucydides being looked upon as a great philosophical historian: philosophy of history & statesmanship, & all that. Saw no signs of it. Read him with admiration as a matchless master of narrative. I agree with Stanley. I think the history of the Sicilian expedition has never been approached.

A Deodara, when finely grown, looks like a green fountain. Humboldt told me that the Himalayan word, really meant (in Sanscrit) 'the timber of the gods'.

When the death of E. Ellice (the Bear) was announced, MaryAnne said 'That is a gentleman, who, according to his own account, has saved or destroyed, every government.'

Henry Lennox, who was a friend of Gladstone & a great admirer, used to say of his speaking, that marvellous as was the performance, both as to voice & volubility, he never said anything, that was ever remembered. There were no 'household words' in his speeches.

   Lord Russell said to me once, speaking of Gladstone, he had 'a wonderful vocabulary'. This was before he was a colleague.

What proves the military spirit of the French is the title of 'Marshal of France'. Every other title has changed from King of France downwards. Even Emperor of France is not permitted. But Marshal of France remains & is highly honored & esteemed.

[53]

G.s.s.* D. said, that he preferred the perfume of fruit to the flavor.

   * Written across the top of the page: 'This was a mem. by George Smythe of some remarks in converson with Mr Disraeli (1873)'.

D. said he thought it a gloomy lot to live during the break up of a revelation.

Which we thought best: commencement of *Iliad* or *Odyssey*? Preferred the latter: higher composition; oftener quoted; πολλῶν δ' ανθρωπων* &c.

Copernican system only a revival; the heliocentric system of Pythagoras; who confessedly derived it from the Egyptians. Galileo invented no system: Gal. a great observer; by nature, & also by the telescope. By abstract thought & constant observation, pursued in serene skies, the ancients in astronomy had anticipated the great results of modern science.

The great inventions of the moderns are in chemistry: at least apparently so.

Very little in metaphysics. Locke's system in Aristotle, as to origin of ideas—very clearly.

Why there was no progress in astronomy for example or rather retrogression was not mere barbarism as commonly said—but introduction into Europe of new ideas: the Semitic mind adopted in Europe brought in the 'firmament' & all that.

That Newton should be born the year Galileo died, good; carrying on the torch.

1864

The Duke of Wellington said, that going to the Opera in state (8 carriages & state liveries) he, as Master of the Horse sitting in the same carriage as the Queen & Prince Consort, the Duke said 'How very ill men look when they smile.'
  'Much worse when they frown' replied Albert.

D. of W.
The Prince had wit. There was a picture at Balmoral; all the chil-

---

* 'Many were the men (whose cities he saw and whose mind he learned...)' Disraeli had mis-spelt the Greek.

dren introduced, game birds &c: one said where is Princess Helena; reply, there with a Kingfisher. 'A very proper bird for a Princess' said Albert.

[54]

Sir George Lewis was a fine scholar, a learned man, an accurate man, & a philosopher—but he was not a profound thinker. He wanted passion for profound thought. His books are like his mind. He was a thorough sceptical speculator. He had formed himself upon Bayle, who had introduced him to a kind of knowledge, unknown to the Universities, & which marked out Lewis from the Gladstones, Lyttletons & all those, who, as far as general knowledge was concerned, were only overgrown schoolboys. 'He knows so much!' John Russell once said to me speaking of Lewis. Bayle is a great bank to draw upon, especially when others do not keep accounts there.

Lord Melbourne was a Baylite. He recommended George Smythe to 'master Bayle'; but George Smythe never took to Bayle. He probably tried Bayle when he was too young.

I gave Stanley Old Audley to read when he was at Hughenden (probably 1856- or 7). I never knew anyone relish anything more keenly. He remarked to me the extraordinary contrast between the vivacity & picturesque details of the mere biographical memoranda, & the vague, prosy narrative of which they were to form the substance, & of which, fortunately for us, old Audley only left a fragment. It was an acute & just criticism. Contrast his enchanting gossip about Hobbes, & the formal character of Hobbes which he afterwards composed.

[55]

1862

Sir George Lewis said to me, at Bellamy's, 'If there be anything established, it is that the Semitic nations invented the alphabet, & after all, that may perhaps be considered the greatest achievement of the human race.' He had been speaking in some depreciation of the Semitic race, in reference to the great inventions of man, when he ended with this observation.

'Of one Semitic nation, the Jews,' I observed, 'it can be said, that they invented alike the Ten Commandments & the Lord's Prayer.'

Sir George Lewis thought the merits of the Lord's Prayer exaggerated. There were expressions in it, which could not be understood by the million, as for instance 'Thy kingdom come' & 'thine is the Kingdom' which, in fact, referred to the impending 'Kingdom of Heaven', which was the foundation of the school of Galilee, & of real Xtianity. I observed that these expressions, though doubtless originally limited in the sense he mentioned, were now of general application, & had always been capable of it. I thought the Lord's Prayer a master-piece. It was the most perfect exponent of the purest religious feeling, that had yet appeared. And while it soothed the cottage, it was difficult to conceive a society so refined, that it would not satisfy.

'Still' he remarked 'it referred to peculiar & temporary circumstances. It was what we should call now a Millenary prayer.'

Speaking of the 'Essays & Reviews' & other works of that kind he said 'There is nothing new in all this. The whole of Neology may be found in an article in Bayle's Dictionary—the article Eve.'

I was surprised at this, being tolerably familiar with Bayle, & on returning home turned to the article Eve—but found nothing of the kind. I mentioned this to Sir George, when I had an opportunity—& he said he would look into the matter. Some days after, we were in the same division lobby, & he told me it was not the article Eve, but some other. He gave me the title, but I forgot it, & meant to have again spoken to him on the subject—when alas! he was no more.

Sir George Lewis, & Lord Melbourne, were both of them great Bayleists.

Sir George Lewis had a remarkable countenance; massy features; antique but not classical; to be found on ancient monuments; it was a Phrygian face. He was rather above middle height. His manner, not his mind—slow. Vast knowledge, & free to communicate. He loved 'talk' as Dr Johnson called it, with a congenial spirit.

[56]

The French Semitic Scholars took the lead at the end of the 17th Century & the beginning of the 18th Century. Père Simon, Astruc, & Bochart—these preceded the German movement. We must not forget Spinoza though—compare dates.

Père Simon's Critical History of the Old Testament was translated by the son of Hampden.

Anthropomorphism: a great cry against it by the Philosophes. But if the Hegelian principle be true, that Man is the first organisation in which God is conscious, then the old legend of Genesis, that God made Man in his own image, comes to the same thing. This is curious, & might be pursued.

Stanley said (1856) I think we shall both live to see a great ecclesiastical crash.

I look upon the Church as the only Jewish Institution remaining. I know no other. A vulgar error to consider circumcision one. That marks them out only in Europe, & not in every part of Europe. If it were not for the Church, I don't see why the Jews should be known. The Church was founded by Jews, & has been faithful to its origin. It secures their history & their literature being known to all Xdom. Every day the Church publickly reads its history, & keeps alive the memory of its public characters; & has diffused its poetry throughout the world. The Jews owe everything to the Church, & are fools to oppose it.

1863

Assuming that the popular idea of Inspiration be abandoned, & the difference between sacred & profane history relinquished, what would be the position of the Hebrew race in universal History, viewed with reference to their influence on Man?

I thought of advertising through a medium that would command confidence £500—or even a £1000 for the best essay on this question; perhaps more precisely expressed. The Judges, perhaps, to be Gladstone, Canon Stanley, & myself. Not bound however to award the prize unless satisfied with the performance.

The History of the Jews is developement or it is nothing. If ever a history were a history of developement, it is that of the Jews.

Talking of old families, & how few took root, Stanley said he thought it was the first two centuries on which it depended. If a family could maintain itself for 200 years, it became so numerous & diffused, that it was difficult, certainly in these times, that it should be extinguished.

Lord Carington said, that all provisions were better in London than in the Country—except butter.

VII

SOCIAL LIFE OF A POLITICAL LEADER

[57]

1863

Comte Apponyi told Lady Salisbury at Hatfield, that he had had an interview respecting Polish affairs with Lord Russell at his private residence, & nothing could be more satisfactory. Lord Russell agreed with him on every point, & that any interference could only redound to the fulfilment of those French views, which were held to be particularly opposed to the interests of England & Austria alike. It was quite agreed, that nothing should induce them to take any step, as the first step, however moderate must lead irresistibly to great embarrassment & mischief. When Comte Apponyi was walking away, the carriage of Baron Gros, the French Ambassador, passed him, & he stopped & watched it to the door of Lord Russell.

The next morning Baron Brunnow, the Russian Ambassador, called upon Comte Apponyi with whom he was on terms of friendship & confidence, & informed Comte Apponyi that interference was decided on, & simultaneous notes were to be written. 'Impossible!' exclaimed Apponyi & he told him what had occurred. Nevertheless in 8 & 40 hours, he found that Brunnow was right.

My father used to say, that Arouet* was the most successful† literary man on record.

Cobden said to me, that the only complete Republic that he knew was the House of Commons.

* ? The name as written by Disraeli is almost indecipherable.
† 'fortunate' written above.

107

Guizot said to me in 1848—the first visit he paid to me after his exile*—'I think your being the Leader of the Tory party is the greatest triumph that Liberalism has ever achieved.'

1844

George Smythe said of Cobden, whom he saw a great [deal] of at Manchester & that district this year, & whom he much admired, that Cobden reminded him of a Saxon Saint. He had that look indeed at that time, meagre—a little melancholy, simple & earnest—but afterwards expanded, & at this moment (1863) may be described as decidedly a stout man, with grey hair, full & rather long. He is rather above the middle size. Cobden was the most persuasive speaker I ever listened to. His voice wanted richness. It was a little too harsh & thin—but his manner was winning. He had great tact, & always conciliated his audience. He was a very amiable man, & extremely well informed. No man entered the House of Commons with a greater prejudice against him among the Country gentlemen, yet in time, he quite overcame it. He was naturally well-bred, because he was considerate for the feelings of others, which is the true course of good breeding. He was modest without being humble—never elated by his great success.

The free trade party subscribed for him a great sum of money: nearly 100,000£ & this was invested in American Securities: Ohio railroads or something of that sort, which turned out very badly, long before the American Civil War. Cobden may be ranked among those great political economists who could manage the affairs of a nation, but not their own. Just before the repeal of the Corn Laws he was on the verge of bankruptcy, & I have been told the preliminary proceedings under such circumstances had commenced. A very few thousands, out of the great sum subscribed, were spared to purchase at Midhurst in Sussex the farm on which he was born & which his father had cultivated. He was passionately fond of this place, & it was curious that his retirement should be in the heart of the Duke of Richmond's country & of those great proprietors & yeomen whom he had particularly assailed. There was no one on the platform, before he entered Parliament, whom Cobden had assailed with such virulence as the

* 'escape' written above.

Duke of Richmond, who was the Leader of the Protectionist party
in the country. The Duke had not spared him. Yet strange to say,
when they had become locally acquainted, which they did in time,
they entertained for each other a great respect & regard. Cobden
was a great favorite among the aristocracy of his neighbourhood.
Lady Dorothy Nevill, who was his neighbour at Dangstein, told
me he was frequently her guest, & the most welcome one, from
his great intelligence & pleasing manners—& that the Duke of
Richmond, & Lord March, & Lord Leconfield—all liked him.

Bright was a great contrast to Cobden. A more powerful
speaker—but not so persuasive. Even when right, he often injured
his cause by his want of the faculty of conciliation. Bright was
a natural & powerful orator. He was Demosthenic. He had
imagination & a glowing soul. Cobden had fancy & was ingeni-
ous. He was not so apt at reply as Cobden, & required more
preparation. This was the consequence of his early & long platform training, in which an oration is always expected. But, on the
whole, he wonderfully adapted himself to the House of Commons,
though on occasions which he deemed great, American slavery for
example, he would sometimes venture on recurring to the platform style—but always failed. The taste of the House of Commons
revolted instantly. Bright, brought up in the most dreadful
prejudices, which he fancied were liberal opinions, & apt to
offend & outrage, was however always learning, & beneath his
apparent vindictiveness & fierceness was a good-hearted man.
Very susceptible of courtesy. He was of the middle height, good-
looking, & wore the Quaker coat as a matter of pride & honor,
though he had quite discarded the religious opinions of the Sect,
or indeed of any other.

[58]

1863

Lady Salisbury told me at Hatfield, that the Bishop of London
(Tait) was, she understood, in much tribulation as to the present
state of religious affairs—not only the victim of perplexity but
the prey of doubt. Thought something serious might happen with
him. The Bishop of Oxford, she told me, was in constant fear of
sudden death: the heart.

Sir Ed. Lytton told me a story many years ago at Knebworth of a furious young Utilitarian, who afterwards, I believe, became an M.P. & even a Minister of State, who was introduced, according to the Whig form with all promising young men, to Holland House, about the time of the Reform Bill. Our friend particularly distinguished by the intense & arrogant self conceit & contempt for others which distinguished [that] but shortlived school, then in its zenith, coolly asked Lord Holland after dinner, apropos of course of something that had preceded, whether His Lordship thought any of the Bishops believed? Upon which Lord Holland went into one of his fits of conversational excitement, spluttered, panted, foamed at the mouth & declared with an air of indignation, that there was immense exaggeration on this subject & that a great many believed. So he began counting the believers on his fingers & he named five or six, but, answering himself all the while remembered that one was dead, was afraid one was a Socinian, another something else, & at last reduced himself to a solitary individual, who 'he was almost sure believed'.

This story was told to Sir Edward by one present whose name he gave me.

Lord Melbourne was very fond of theology. I do not know what would have happened to him, if he had lived to become acquainted with the Neologic School. A few years before his death, & before his illness, he rode over from Brocket to a Herts. neighbour, Mr Blake a celebrated man of Science & of estate & who had once been mentioned as President [of the] Royal Society —I believe even offered that post—the friend & equal of Wollaston, Davy, & all of that time. Lord Melbourne, who was on terms of great intimacy with him & highly regarded him, wished to converse with him alone—& it was on the subject of a future state. 'I wish' said Lord Melbourne 'to put the question to you not in a religious, but a purely scientific, light. Do you believe in the possibility of a future life?'

'Answering you strictly as a man of Science, & guarding myself, as you properly have done from any religious opinion, I have no hesitation in saying, that I think it utterly impossible.'

Upon which Melbourne gave a shrug & a groan, ordered his horse & galloped home.

Social Life of a Political Leader

[59]

1863

Bishop of Oxford sent this year to Switzerland; overworked. Certainly no man was ever so busy: preached more sermons, wrote more letters, attended more platform meetings, or infused, generally, such a spirit in his diocese.

I think his present illness however is from chagrin. He never recovered [from] the appointment of Dr. Thomson to York. It was a long time vacant, & he was my guest at Hughenden during the interval. I never knew a man more agitated. It was the height of his ambition. I think he would have preferred it to Canterbury. He was a Yorkshireman; the son of a great Yorkshireman, who had represented the undivided County of York, & had fairly won it. It was known, that no more Low Church Bishops were to be appointed. That vein had been overworked. Some of the last appointments in that way had been mean & insignificant. The death of the Prince had checked the hopes of the Broad Church which were once very high. The Prince had managed to push one in, & had intended to have made the Queen insist on Dr. Temple, but the subsequent publication of 'Essays & Reviews' to which he was the leading contributor would probably have rendered this impossible. The death of the Prince was a great check to the Broad Church. He had made Stanley & Kingsley already Chaplains.

As Lord Shaftesbury, the great champion of Low Church & maker of Low Church Bishops, was, it was understood, to lie by a little, & as Broad Church was from public feeling impossible, the Bishop of Oxford thought that Gladstone, who was his greatest friend & for whom he had left his natural political allies, would have insisted on his appointment to York. If Gladstone had threatened to resign as he did about the Paper Duty, he must have gained his point. But Gladstone made no sign, & a comparatively young Oxonian, at least 15 years younger, I should think than the Bishop of Oxford, &, if of any political opinions, a Tory, was appointed—an excellent appointment in my opinion, but that does not alter the circumstances.

Lord Palmerston had an extraordinary good fortune, apparently, in his Church patronage. The three Primacies of Canterbury,

York & Armagh, all fell vacant in the same year, & our party were loud in their laments over our ill-luck & the just disappointment of our friends. Now it so happened that Lord Palmerston's party resources were quite exhausted. Lord Shaftesbury for several years his guide on Church matters had scandalised the Country by some of his late low Church appointments; the death of the Prince & public feeling had arrested the Broad Church; & if the Tories had been in power, they would have probably appointed the very three individuals whom he was obliged to choose—

Longley to Canterbury
Thomson to York
&
Beresford to Armagh.

This last appointment was loudly cried against by the Liberal party & I doubt whether we could have dared to do it, but Lord Palmerston was then coquetting with the Irish Prots.

A Beresford!—& succeeding a Beresford. It was thought strong. The upshot is we lost nothing in these matters by being in opposition.

[60]

1863

Old Lady Tankerville (Lady Palmerston's greatest friend; had hunted in couples with her in their youth, & long after) was reproaching Lady Palmerston this year for having changed her party &c. 'If you had been less ambitious, you might have done a great deal for all your old friends.'

Lady Pam said with a sort of impudent, prim, look, which she could put on 'Well; I have got what I wanted.'

Lady William Powlett used to say of a man, that he had fallen into vanity—not that he had fallen in love. She would say 'Mr —— has fallen into vanity with Lady Augusta' and she had known a good deal about these things.

1863

Looking out of the windows at the great Hall at Hatfield this year
with Lord Clanwilliam (who had lived much abroad (diplomatic-
ally & otherwise) & in the great seats of war) & beholding the
unrivalled scene of its kind—the terraces, rich gardens—fountains
& flowers—& then the fine old park with its vast trees & colossal
fern 'What strikes me' he said 'in this scene is here is a country,
which has never known the conqueror's hoof.'

Lord Grenville used to say the three great Englishmen were
Bacon, Milton, & Newton.
    Telling this to Stanley, he remarked with a grim, &, I think,
not displeased smile 'Then Shakespeare went for nothing?' The
Stanleys had no imagination—but Lord Derby, if he had a passion,
had one for Shakespeare & when he was quite alone with his
family, especially at Knowsley, used to read S aloud every night.
    When we were discussing any grave point—especially on
affairs, & Stanley saw nothing but difficulties, & I evinced any
impatience he used to say 'I know what you are going to say, I
know what you are going to say.' He meant, that he had no
imagination—and sometimes when I said so, he would reply 'I
knew you would say that.'

The mania of Francis Egerton during the last years of his life was
that he should die in a workhouse.
    I fancy this is a disease peculiar to very rich men. Morrison,
who was in parliament when I first entered, & who, from a shop
boy, had risen to the head of Todd, Morrison & Co., & died
worth, I believe, four millions, received during the last years of
his life twelve shillings a week from his bailiff for working in his
own garden at Basildon. He was otherwise sensible enough; at
least quite harmless.
    Morrison bought Basildon Park & the estate from Sir Francis
Sykes. I passed there in 34 & 35 some romantic hours. It was one
of those rich sylvan scenes, that abound in the valley of the
Thames; & the house a Palladian palace. M. gave for the estate
140,000.

[61]

August: 1863

The 'Honorable Robert J. Walker; M.A. Counsellor at Law in the Supreme Court of the United States; late Law Rep. Mi., Senator of the United States, Secretary of the Treasury, Commissioner to China, Governor of Kansas &c &c' sent me the copy of a pamphlet today entitled 'Jefferson Davis & Repudiation &c &c' an attack upon the President of the Confederate States. Before I left town, I was informed by a Cabinet Minister (Charles Villiers) that this Mr Walker was to be the next President of the U.S.; that it was all arranged; & that he would be carried by the Democratic Unionist Party.

It is a strange & singular fact, that at the last meeting of the Standing Committee of the Trustees of the British Museum, at which I was present, this 'Hon. Robt J. Walker' was reported as having abused his permission to use the Reading Room & having mis-appropriated a rare pamphlet on early American politics. His conduct after detection was worse, if possible, than the act itself. He had been introduced by the American Minister, or rather Secretary of the American Mission. Walker pretended through that medium, that he had written to the Principal Librarian of the B.M. on the subject fully: no letters ever arrived; then that he had sent to America to get from some public Library a copy of the missing work; then that he would reprint it at his own expense, & other random excuses & expedients used by persons who had compromised themselves. Finally, when I left town, he appeared to have taken refuge in silence & general disregard of the matter. I shall watch with interest the next election of President of the U.S.

1863

In my first audience of the Queen this year after the death of the Prince Consort, the Queen among other things spoke to me of the state of the British Museum of which I had just been elected a trustee in succession to Lord Lansdowne. H.M. asked me what I thought of Panizzi? and whether he were equal to the post.

I replied that my official experience was too slight to permit me to offer a personal opinion, but that he was much esteemed by my colleagues.

H.M. thought it strange that a foreigner should be at the head of an Institution so peculiarly national.

I observed, that the post had been frequently filled by foreigners; that when I was a boy it was filled by Mr Planta, a Swiss, & the father of a gentleman who had served her Majesty's uncles as Under Secretary of State for Foreign Affairs: that in olden days Dr. Maty, who, I believe, was a Frenchman, had been in high office at the Museum, & I mentioned also Baber, though I was not so clear about him. I mentioned also that Mr Hallam thought very highly of Panizzi, & that my father, a great authority on vernacular literature, had been astonished by his intimate acquaintance with English books.

[62]

1863—Augt.

Lady Carington noticed the extraordinary change of manners, & want of courtesy that prevailed; defended by greater ease in society &c. &c. Her mother Lady Willoughby always rose whenever any body called on her; now men often do not rise when ladies enter a room. Her mother almost the only lady who invariably rose, & had taught her the same habit. Old Duchess of Gloucester rose to the last. Mr. Sneyd, *vieille cour* to his finger ends, called on H.R.H. & she rose from her seat to welcome him. He could not refrain at last from venturing to express his surprise, that H.R.H. should disturb herself to welcome him, & said that he had just left a Duchess, & not a Royal Duchess, who never moved either when he entered or retired. 'Mr Sneyd' H.R.H. replied 'I have been brought up to show my sense of the kindness of those, who honor me by their society.'

Lord Willoughby de Eresby was equally punctilious, though otherwise very simple & easy in his manners. 'Now if Eva ever (her daughter & his granddaughter) were to enter the room, my father would rise from his seat; I am not by any means sure that Eva, if he entered, would.' Eva was only 16, & very pretty.

The two most successful dramatic writers were both actors: Molière & Shakespeare.

Quoting one day from the Gospels, Eliot Yorke said it was very strange, that the two great exponents of human thought & feeling were the persons of whom we had the least knowledge. 'We know, if possible, less' he added 'of Shakespeare, than of Jesus.'

Looking at a portrait of Southey, Hobhouse (Lord Broughton) said 'That man failed from want of knowledge of the world.'

It is a curious thing, that all the great financial lights, whose writings were at the time constantly quoted, & whose opinions no doubt influenced the great commercial changes, were all bankrupts. McCulloch the Secretary of the board of Trade was a bankrupt hatter, George Porter the head of the Statistical Department was a bankrupt wine-merchant. Tooke the author of 'History of Prices' was turned out of the Commercial House in which he was a partner, in consequence of his speculations in tallow. Wilson, Secretary of the Treasury, & afterwards Financial Minister in India, was a bankrupt hatter.

There was a pompous noisy writer, who imitated Burke & Cobbett, & was an oracle of the Country gentlemen for a time in 1843–7 as Editor & chief & only writer of the *Banker's Circular*, which Newdegate really thought inspired. He turned out to be one Burges; once a wool broker, of the firm of Burges & Hubbard, who had also been in the Gazette, a quarter of a century before.

When Fullarton, a great East Indian fortune, suddenly crashed from what was supposed a pecuniary position of colossal supremacy, he took to writing on the currency, & was the only writer, whom Peel feared & whom Lord Overstone thought it necessary to answer. He was the fashionable authority for some time in Parliament among a certain set of young & clever men; such as Charles Buller, Benjamin Hawes.

At the time of the currency debates, Charles Buller said to me 'I swear by Fullarton.'

[63]

On Saturday* 15th August 1863, coming home from dining with
Lord & Lady Carington at Wycombe Abbey—about eleven
o'clock—MaryAnne called my attention to some brilliant sparks
on the window of the carriage—& which we at first thought were
reflected from the lamps on some marks in the glass—but we
immediately observed that they moved & darted about. Letting
down the window, the glittering bodies remained. They were
fire-flies! They seemed like small moths. As we were ascending
the hill in Hughenden park, which is steep, we did not like to stop
the carriage, which I have ever regretted. They followed us the
whole way, till we arrived at the gate entering the pleasure
grounds, which were quite dark. The servants said they saw nothing when we spoke to them on our arrival—but servants never
observe.

We resolved to go the next night, about the same hour, in a
carriage, to secure the attraction of the lamps & with 'witnesses',
as MaryAnne said, but the next night it rained, & the weather
altogether changed, which for many weeks had been singularly
fine & hot.

We told all this to our friends, but always with the reservation,
that we did not expect anyone to believe us, as fire-flies have
never been heard of in such a latitude.

1860

I find great amusement in talking to the people at work in the
woods & grounds at Hughenden. Their conversation is racy, &
the repose of their natural manners agreeable. An old, but very
hale, man told me today, that he was going to be married, & that
his bride would not be much younger than himself, but he had
lodged in her cottage now for more than a year, & he thought she
would do for him. He said he was a widower, & he added, speaking of his first wife, '& I can truly say, from the bottom of my
heart, that for fifty years, I never knew what it was to have a
happy hour'.

I told my wife of this, & they are to have a wedding dinner. I
like very much the society of woodmen. Their conversation is

* Written above: 'This aftds explained'.

most interesting—quick & constant observation, & perfect knowledge. I don't know any men, who are so completely masters of their business, & of the secluded, but delicious world in which they live. They are healthy. Their language is picturesque; they live in the air, & Nature whispers to them many of her secrets. A Forest, is like the Ocean, monotonous only to the ignorant. It is a life of ceaseless variety.

To see Lovett, my head-woodman fell a tree is a work of art. No bustle, no exertion, apparently not the slightest exercise of strength. He tickles it with his axe; & then it falls exactly where he desires it. He can climb a tree like a squirrel, an animal, which, both in form & color & expression, he seems to me to resemble.

[64]

Octr 13 1863

Lord Lyndhurst died this morning. He had a mind equally distinguished for its vigor & flexibility. He rarely originated, but his apprehension was very quick & he mastered the suggestions of others & made them clearer & more strong. He had a great grasp—thoroughly mastered a subject; deep & acute; & sometimes when you thought him slow, was only exhaustive. In his statements accurate, complete, & singularly lucid: the clearest mind on affairs with equal power of conceiving & communicating his perspicuous views.

His soul wanted ardor for he was deficient in imagination, though by no means void of sensibility. He adapted himself to circumstances in a moment though he could not create, or even considerably control them. His ambition active, not soaring. Its natural height to hold the great seal *thrice*: but when the King in 1836 had it conveyed to him that he might be called upon to take the first place, & would he be ready, he exclaimed 'why, I am a lawyer not a statesman' & seemed disconcerted—but when he had talked over the matter with a friend,* he not only arrived at the result that he was a statesman, but let his Majesty be assured

---

* '(i.e. D. 1873)' written above.

LORD LYNDHURST

'His countenance was that of a high-bred falcon'

EDWARD LYTTON
BULWER

'the vainest man that perhaps ever existed'

LORD GEORGE BENTINCK
'very firm to me'

THE FOURTEENTH
EARL OF DERBY
'he had no imagination'

SIR ROBERT PEEL
'he died cheering me'

LORD PALMERSTON
'What an impudent fellow!'

QUEEN VICTORIA AND THE PRINCE CONSORT

'he *would* die'

that he was prepared to do his bidding, though it was one unusually difficult & perilous.

His cultivation was considerable: far more than he was given credit for. His reading had been various & extensive, though he never sought to display it, & his scientific acquirements notable. He retained & digested everything; supported by a powerful & well ordered memory.

A pleader rather than an orator, & never a debater. Unsuccessful in the House of Commons, he rose at once in the House of Lords to a position of unapproached supremacy; the times were favorable to him there. His stately & luminous expositions, in a voice of thrilling music, were adapted to a senate of which he caught the tone with facility. His taste almost amounted to austerity, yet he did not appreciate Demosthenes, & was a strong Ciceronian.

He had a sweet disposition, with a temper that nothing could ruffle; indulgent, placable, free from prejudice & utterly devoid of vanity. His feelings perhaps were not very strong, but they were always kind.

His mind was playful, but not witty, & he had little humor though he could sympathise with it. His knowledge of mankind was great, but not consummate, for in their management, there was this error, he was willing to give them credit for being influenced by amiable, but not elevated feelings.*

He was wonderfully fond of the society of women & this not merely from his susceptibility to the sex, which was notorious, but because he was fond of them in every relation of life. He loved to be surrounded by his family who were all females: a mother of 90, a sister nearly his own age, & who survived him in the possession of all her faculties, indulged & devoted daughters. He was happy in two marriages, though his wives in every respect were very different. His person was highly prepossessing. Far above the middle height, his figure was symmetrical & distinguished, & though powerfully formed, he never became stout. His countenance was that of a high-bred falcon. Indeed nothing could be finer than the upper part of his countenance. His deepset eye gleamed with penetrating fire & his brow was majestic. Nothing could be more beautiful. It was that of the Olympian Jove. The

---

* This paragraph is boxed off in the manuscript; perhaps Disraeli intended to omit or alter it, or to change its position.

lower part of his countenance betrayed the deficiencies of his character; a want of high purpose, & some sensual attributes.*

[65]

Lytton said to me once on our bench in the House 'What strikes me most singular in you is, that you are fonder of Power than of Fame.'

Three great men who rouged:
> Lytton
> Palmerston
> Lyndhurst.

Lady Tankerville asked Lord Lyndhurst, whether he believed in Platonic Friendship?

'After, but not before' was the reply.

On the death of Lord George Bentinck, the leadership of the Opposition was placed in commission—Herries, Lord Granby & myself. George Smythe took the news to his old chief, Lord Aberdeen who said with one of his grim smiles 'Sieyès, Roger Ducos & Napoleon Bonaparte'.†

[66]

Geo. Smythe was very rich when he had made up his mind to marry an heiress, & gave his instructions to all the ladies who were, & who had been, in love with him, to work for his benefit. 'Family' he used to say 'I don't care the least for: would rather

---

* After this paragraph are the following rough notes, in pencil:
'How he shrank and shrivelled the last years like Metth. Lord Melbourne his great opponent and greatest admirer always addressed him in affection as the true aristocrat.
L.
Manners. Gleams of want of refinement from early associations, when the females were not ladies, and having entered polished society late. Nearer 50 than 40.'

† '; we know how that will end' was the original conclusion, later crossed out.

like to marry into a rich, vulgar, family. Madness, no objection. As for scrofula, why should I care for it more than a King? All this ought to be a great pull in my favor.' Strange to say, he succeeded & married an heiress—but literally on his death-bed.

Lord Lyndhurst used to say, when a celebrity disappeared 'No one is ever missed.'

The Duke of Wellington said of Peel 'That is a gentleman, who never sees the end of a campaign.'

Peel said of the Duke of Wellington, who had changed his previous view on some course, on which they had agreed 'Just like him; the last man who has his ear, always has him.'

These are authentic traits. The person who told me, was the individual, in both instances, to whom the remarks were made.

Lady Waldegrave (Braham, the singer's daughter) said to Madame de Rothschild 'I am a true Jewess; I love curiosities & I love Dukes.'

Brunnow said to me at Court in 1860, speaking of the Emperor of the French 'I give him five years.'

I made this memorandum in 1863 (Octr).

[67]

Gladstone said (1864) that the invasion of Mexico by the Emperor Napoleon was one of the greatest political blunders ever perpetrated; certainly, the greatest political blunder of his time.

But note: there never was a political move over which the Emperor had so long & so deeply brooded—for many years. In 1857 he mentioned to me his wish & willingness to assist in establishing a European dynasty in Mexico, & said that for his part he would make no opposition to the accession of the Duc d'Aumale to such a throne. He looked upon its establishment, as of high European importance.

It was his custom to say, that there were two powers who hated old Europe: Russia & the U.S. of America.

Stanley said (1857) that science disqualified one for public life:

the whole thing seemed so small (speaking of our globe) that it required a great effort to treat affairs seriously.

Said that he heard a great deal of the political wisdom to be found in Thucydides: a study for statesmen &c &c—first philosophical historian & all that. For his part never could find it out: what he did find was a matchless narrative.

[68]

Augt. 5 1864

Long walk in the park with Brunnow—spoke much of Bismarck. I reminded him, he had introduced Bis. to me at a ball at his Chesham house two years ago; which he recollected. We agreed —a man of great energy—'An Alberoni' I added.

Brunnow doubted, whether circumstances had favored Alberoni, as they had Bis. Thought there was no person whom circumstances ever so favored. France holding back, because she was offended with England; English Government in a state of 'impuissance'; Russia distracted with conflicting interests; Austria for the first time sincere in wishing to act with Prussia; then the weak chivalric character of the King; the enthusiasm of Germany.

'Bismarck made a good book' I said.

'He made a good book & what is most strange he backed the worst horse in the lot. For Prussia is a country without any bottom, & in my opinion could not maintain a real war for 6 months.'

I reminded Brunnow of what he had said about Louis Napoleon (the five years). He accepted it: 'I gave him originally 15 years from 1850 I think. Well the lease approaches its term.'

[69]

1864

It is said that Lord Derby has paid off the whole debt left by his father, which was large, above half a million, & has considerably more than £100,000 per annum. He has only one country seat to keep up, Knowsley, which would be the ugliest house in England, were it not for his 'family mansion' in St. James's Square. That is furnished like a second-rate lodging house, & is in itself essentially mean: all this not from stinginess, but from sheer want of taste. His entertainments are sufficient & splendid as regards plate, wines & cookery: both of which latter are 1st rate: his stable first rate both in town & country. No one has more splendid horses & equipages than Lady Derby. He looks after this. She with a weakness for 'great folks' seems never to catch anything of the taste & splendor of their lives. 'Did you ever see such china in a room' exclaimed Lady Chesterfield. 'It's what you would put in your stillroom in the country.'

1864

Speaking at the end of the Session, when the Danish business was pretty well over, Charles Villiers (a Cabinet Minister) said 'he believed that the Emperor of the French was really afraid of Germany. He was haunted by the idea of the revival of the Coalition.'

The first meeting of Lord & Lady Palmerston was at the Opera. Lady Palmerston then Countess Cowper was at the Opera with old Lady Granville (the mother of the Lord President). Lady Palmerston said more than once to Lady Granville 'Who is that very good-looking young man, who keeps looking at me?—I wonder who is that very good-looking young man with Mr —— & who keeps looking at me.' I forget now, whether Lady Granville knew Lord Palmerston or not; I am inclined to think not. Lord Palmerston was in the alley beneath with his companion whom both ladies knew. In about ten minutes' time, they entered the box, & his friend, whose name I can't recall, introduced Lord Pam to Countess Cowper. Lady Granville told this to my informant.

It was love at first sight: a grand passion. After a time, the usual consequences ensued. There were recriminations & mutual reproaches of infidelity and they separated—& for some time. Then Lord Pam's sister (I think Mrs. Bowes), to whom he was much attached, & who was the soul of the family, died, & Lord

Palmerston shut himself up & quite retired from society. And then Lady Cowper wrote a letter of condolence to him, & he called upon her & all was renewed, & notwithstanding occasional scenes &c. terminated in that celebrated alliance, to which he owes in a great degree his success.

[70]

1864

Stanley said of Lord Derby 'My father has no intimates except the sharers of his amusements.' Said his father, as he was now greatly incapacitated from taking those amusements, found some relief in translating the *Iliad*, which he intended to complete.

Aberdeen & Palmerston were at Harrow together, & Palmerston was three months the elder. This particularly annoyed Aberdeen when Palmerston alluded to him in the House of Commons as 'a piece of antiquated imbecility'. He said half playfully 'The impudent fellow! Why I'm his junior by three months.'

1864

The Session a very curious one; I was watching for five months for the proper moment for battle. It was very difficult to restrain out friends. The Government every day more unpopular, yet it was clear to me that the House would not directly censure them. The tactic was to postpone to the last moment a direct attack, but to defeat them in the interval on some indirect vote, taking advantage of the discontent of the House. Thus on the Ashantee war we ran them to 6 or 7 & on Stansfeld's affair to 10: on either question, they would have resigned. On the direct vote* their majority was 18, of which they affected to be proud, though in old days, it would have been considered a defeat. Sir Robert Peel on his vote of want of confidence in 1840 moved by Sir John Buller was beaten by 22—but was Minister next year 1841.

Lord Palmerston after the division scrambled up a wearying staircase to the ladies' gallery. My informant, who was behind him,

* '(Their Danish policy. 1873)' written above.

had the good taste & tact to linger. He saw the ladies' gallery open & Lady Palmerston advance & they embraced! An interesting scene & what pluck—to mount those dreadful stairs at three o'clock in the morning & 80 years of age! My informant would not disturb them. It was a great moment! But silly Lady de Grey who with other Whig ladies was in the gallery with Lady Palmerston would come forward with 'O! dear Lord Palmerston! How nice!' &c &c, which spoilt all.

VIII

GENTLEMAN OF HUGHENDEN

Old Lord Tankerville used to say 'A great country house is a very equivocal luxury.' He was very amusing describing the details of the results of a great reception of one's friends at a château— no doubt from the remembrances of Chillingham 'and when they had all gone & you rode about your fields, you found a parcel of dead & wounded birds—& they gone to town perhaps to say it was "damned bad shooting".'

Lady Desart said the ball at —— House was dull. There was a want of young men. 'For a ball to go off well' she said 'you must have the dancing dogs.'

The parentage of the new French Ambassador, Baron Gros, was said to be doubly royal. He was a son of Charles the 10th by the Duchess of Bourbon.

The Queen asked me the real difference between the two great Exhibitions 1851—& 1862. I ventured to say 'The first was a Woman; the second a Man.'

Lady Carington said, & justly, that Lady Jersey was the only person in England, who had ever succeeded in establishing a 'salon'. All the great ladies had tried it, & all had failed. It requires the acme of social position, knowledge, & tact—great self command. If a bore comes, & however inopportune, you must never by your reception of him let him suspect that he is a bore, or he will go about, & tell, & prevent others coming. For a *salon* must not be a *clicque*. That many may command, & most end in who try *salon*. But to be at home every evening requires great sacrifice—but it was no sacrifice to Lady Jersey. She delighted in it. Society was her passion, & she had every quality to make it agreeable. Inexhaustible animation, unrivalled tact, & no wish to show off.

Madame Flahault was at home every night, but it was a clicque— Old Pahlen, the old Bear & three or four others. There might be new gossip, but no new views or feeling. Like a club in the *Spectator* & those papers.

Lord Foley used to say, (& he was a very delicate looking man— a gourmand & a Sybarite, but manly & grand seigneur) when they talked to him of things agreeing or disagreeing &c. 'I should like to see my stomach presume to refuse digesting anything I chose to put into it.'

Lord George Bentinck had no wardrobe. He had always a complete new suit of clothes on a chair in his bedroom.

The old Duke of Portland never communicated with his family except by writing.

I have a passion for books & trees. I like to look at them. When I come down to Hughenden I pass the first week in sauntering about my park & examining all the trees, & then I saunter in the library, & survey the books. My collection is limited to Theology, the Classics, & History. Anything miscellaneous in it is the remains of the Bradenham Collection; but the great bulk of the Belles Lettres, I parted with after my father's death. It was sold by Sotheby.

[72]

The Earl of Mornington, dying, comparatively speaking, young —40 or 45—has left his estate to his second cousin, Earl Cowley, our Ambassador at Paris, who had risen to an earldom without a shilling. This was a wise piece of fortune. The estate will in time be not less than ten thousand a year, but there is at present a capital House, well-appointed & three thousand a year clear to spend. The Cowleys delighted. I believe the whole of the shooting over the vast mortgaged estates of Long Pole Wellesley is also

Lord Cowley's, who is to give up Chantilly & spend all his holidays in England.

Lady Cowley says the house is delightful (Draycot?), not too large—but everything they could wish; everything ready, carriages, horses, everything. Among other things fifty thousand cigars of high quality. I suppose by this, that Lord Mornington smoked himself to death. I met him once, half a dozen years ago, at Paris, at dinner at Lord Cowley's. He seemed to me a sickly, half-developed frame. However he has made a very proper will. Lady Cowley affects immense astonishment, but I believe they looked after him—& I think, quite rightly.

This estate was the debris of the great Tylney Long Estates. When the late Lord Mornington joined with his father the profligate Long Wellesley, & raised more than $\frac{1}{2}$ a million to pay his father's debts, this estate was settled on him as the consideration. I knew Long Pole Wellesley; of course after his fall. He had been living years at Brussels when the death of his father permitted him to return to England as Earl of Mornington. He was still handsome, his hair quite white, with black eye brows, & the most piercing eyes I ever saw. This is organic, I believe, with the Wellesleys. At least the Marquess was so, & Dr Wellesley the Principal of some Hall at Oxford, whom I sat next to at dinner at College, (guest of the V. Chancellor) when the Prince of Wales dined there this year, & who was a son of Lord Wellesley, was the same (Dr Wellesley, by the bye, a man of high cultivation, fine taste & scholarship—a dignus filius).

Lord Mornington was one of the wickedest looking men I ever saw. There was an audacious recklessness in his glance. He rather wanted height—at least, he had become corpulent. I had some conversation with him, but his talk was rather audacious than clever. I met him at Lady Blessington's.

The present Duke of Wellington was very kind to him & at first he floated, attended the House of Lords & all that—but I have heard that his credit being quite exhausted, he intrenched himself at last in his lodgings in Mount Street which he would never quit, from the fear of the door being shut in his face when he returned, & passed his life entirely in smoking. When his stock of cigars was exhausted, I suppose, he died. And his son died leaving fifty thousand behind him. What a dialogue between the father & son in the Elysian fields!

A Duke of Bedford (I believe Francis the Agricultural Duke) dining one day at the Lord Mayor's had for a neighbour a gentleman whom he did not know, but to whom he was courteous. Among other things, the gentleman had no servant, & the Duke who was attended, desired his servant to attend equally to the gentleman. In the true English [manner] they separated, mutually pleased, without the Duke ascertaining his companion's name. Next morning, the gentleman called at Bloomsbury House, then the palace of the Russells. He was the Earl of Tilney, an Irish Earl, who, I believe, had been long out of England, & was not known in general society. He came to acknowledge the great courtesy of the Duke by which he was evidently deeply gratified. The acquaintance thus formed, was to a certain degree cultivated. It was easy for the Duke to pay Lord Tilney other social attentions, which were highly appreciated—& Lord Tilney made his will, & left the whole of his vast estates to the Duke of Bedford.

Some time after this: it may have been years, the Duke of Bedford who was a very passionate man, coming home found the Court-yard at Bloomsbury House full of cases addressed to the Earl of Tilney, care of His Grace, the Duke of Bedford, Bloomsbury House. These were choice marble & antiquities collected by the Earl in Italy. The Duke was in such a passion at this liberty taken with him by his Lord Mayor's dinner protegé, that he either wrote, or directed to be written to Lord Tilney on the subject, who was informed that Bloomsbury House was not a warehouse.

Whereupon Lord Tilney removed the goods, & altered his will, & left his vast estates—among them the famous Wanstead House, the palace probably which these marbles were to adorn, in such limitations, that they ultimately came to that unhappy & celebrated heiress, Miss Tylney Long, who married Wellesley, eldest son of Lord Maryborough & nephew of the Duke of Wellington—& who made such memorable ducks & drakes of her almost unrivalled inheritance.

The late Duke of Bedford told this story to my friend & neighbour, Lord Carington, Lord Lieutenant of the County of Bucks., who told it to me.

The late Duke of Bedford was a very good man, with a sense of duty, which he endeavoured to fulfil, but he was singularly avaricious. What pain the remembrance of this lost inheritance must have cost him! The late Duke of Bedford was very much alarmed about the consequences of the Repeal of the Corn Laws, & to the very last indulged in the hope of a fixed duty. He was a great friend of the late Duke of Rutland, a Tory & Protectionist. They corresponded frequently—perhaps two or three times a week. When I was at Belvoir Castle in 1846–7–8, the Duke of Rutland often read me passages from the Duke of Bedford's letters on the agricultural situation which was then critical. Besides this subject, he was most engrossed by the state of his income. His father, (the son of Francis the agricultural Duke) had left a large debt; about a million sterling. The late Duke when he acceded was panic-struck—& even sold his father's cellar of wines, who then lived in Belgrave Square. But when he looked about him a little, he found he was not quite ruined, & at the time of this correspondence, though his father could not have been dead 20 years, his excitement was to reach, by way of income, the sum of £200,000 per annum. He mentioned this frequently in his letters to the late Duke of Rutland, who showed to me, or rather read to me a passage, in which the Duke of Bedford said, that he calculated by Xmas two years, he would realize this great result. I understand he did so, & then he died, his mission being fulfilled.

It was thought he would have provided handsomely for Lord John Russell, to whom he had been political advisor all his life, & who, by his advice, & with his sanction, had sought from the Crown the dignity of an Earldom. But he left Lord John, only an Irish estate—of no great amount, which had been left the Duke of Bedford by an Earl Ludlow, another Irish Earl—but alas! not a Tylney. I don't think Earl Russell got more than three or four thousand a year by this legacy. The world thought, that with his vast means, the Duke ought to have established this branch. A friend of mine was staying at Woburn. The party had retired for the night, but my friend who had left a letter of some importance on a card table, returned to the saloon suddenly & unexpectedly, & found the Duke of Bedford, mounted on a chair, & putting out the lights of the central Chandelier!

When the Duke of Portland, who was a Minister, died, his debts were so vast, & his embarrassments so complicated, that it was thought the Bentinck family were finished. The late Duke of Portland, then a young man, sold Bulstrode which was the chief seat (*not estate*) of the family, & which had him as Marquess of

Titchfield Member for the County of Buckingham—he killed all
the deer, & buried them at night, for the Bentincks were too
proud to sell their deer, & a system of severe retrenchment was
established & pursued. That Duke of Portland (the late Duke)
lived to an advanced age, & in the enjoyment of fine health. At
eighty, he had not lost a tooth. He died almost as rich as the Duke
of Bedford. He left 180,000 per annum & he was not a niggard,
but a man capable of magnificent acts of generosity. Talking of
expenditure once, His Grace said 'Well I don't [know] how they
manage, but I never could get at the bottom of five & twenty
thousand a year.'

These are two instances of the difficulty of destroying a family
rooted in the land. I have seen several instances of this in my time.
The late Duke of Buckingham had never a rental, like the Bed-
fords & the Bentincks. That house, from a plain country gentleman, (but a very ancient family, for they were established in
Bucks. & were High Sheriffs in the times of the Plantagenets) had
built themselves up by marrying heiresses—the heiresses of Lord
Cobham which gave them Stowe; of the Earl Nugent which
gave them a large Irish estate; of the last Duke of Chandos which
gave them 7 & twenty thousand a year in Essex, Midex, Somerset-
shire &c. but their rent-roll never exceeded 65 thousand per
annum (sixty five). I think their patrimonial estate, Wotton,
the real Grenville estate, was about fourteen thousand per
annum.

And this sixty five thousand, they never had clear, for they had
been since the days of Lord Temple & Wilkes an expensive &
embarrassed family.

(Mem. the late Duke of Bucks who married for love & who was
the first who had not married an heiress ultimately by a quirk of
Scotch Law, which he never dreamed of when he wedded, got
140,000 by his wife Lady Mary Campbell, & sister of the Marquess of Breadalbane.)

The crash of the Grenville family seemed conclusive. The late
Duke owed two millions. The present Duke, then Lord Chandos,
had joined his father in cutting off the entail of the Buckingham
estates, 40,000 per annum, without any provision for himself, &
had intended to have done the same with regard to the Chandos—
but it was found they were not entailed, but conveyed to trustees
for life interests, so that he could only part with his life, & that of

his son, if he had one, would be preserved. This led to delays & negotiations & lawyers being called in, & certain insurances to a great amount, £300,000, which the father had intended to have converted into money, were kept up for the benefit of the son. The pictures & plate & splendid curiosities of Stowe were sold by auction. Lord Chandos took the post of paid Chairman of the Great North Western Railway—& yet, at this moment, fifteen years having elapsed, the Duke of Buckingham is living at Stowe, which is partially furnished, & at Wotton, which is entirely kept up—with five & twenty thousand per annum.

Then again Lord Lichfield is a remarkable case of the entire revival of a family, supposed not twenty years ago to be irretrievably ruined. Lord Chesterfield another—even said now to be getting rich by coal mines.

Lord Foley *was* rooted out of the land—but when all was paid, there was a surplus of several hundred thousand pounds. Lord Foley has twelve thousand a year—the best appointed house & equipages in London, & has recently purchased an estate in Notts.—part of that famous Worksop which belonged to the Duke of Norfolk, the father of Lady Foley.

Lord Foley told me that Worksop Manor, a chef d'oeuvre, was pulled down in a panic from the Duke of Norfolk thinking his pecuniary position very bad. They now receive a clear sixty thousand per annum from their northern estates of which Worksop Manor House was the becoming seat! And deeply regret a blunder of not a quarter of a century ago!

Mem. that Lord Ward gave the largest *fancy* price for Lord Foley's estate Whitley Court yet known. But this does not affect my position that it is difficult if not impossible to ruin a family well rooted in the Land. It rather confirms it, for *fancy* price is one of the incidents of that peculiar property.

[73]

1865

At Court; a renewed rumor that the Emperor of the French was seriously ill. Some one said to Brunnow 'But what is his complaint?' 'That' replied the Russian Ambassador, 'which killed my late master, & so many of his predecessors. No one can stand it. The responsibility of arbitrary power.'

I heard him say this.

1865

At the meeting of the House this year when I went up to salute the Speaker, I asked particularly after his health: he had had a severe attack in the autumn. 'I am all right' said the Speaker 'but how is your great man? How is Lord Derby? I dined with the other yesterday, according to custom, as you know. I have had the honor too of dining at your right hand. Well yesterday, there was a young man (he is coming into the house now in scarlet uniform—Hanbury Tracy, who was to second the address) who sate on my left & I said to him at the end of the dinner "Now you are a very young man, & if I were you when I went home tonight I would make a memorandum of what happened to day; something in this fashion—Mem. dined with the Prime Minister, who was upwards of 80 years of age. He ate for dinner two plates of turtle-soup; he was then served very amply to a plate of cod & oyster sauce; he then took a paté; afterwards he was helped to two very greasy-looking entrées; he then despatched a plate of roast mutton; there then appeared before him the largest, & to my mind, the hardest, slice of ham that ever figured on the table of a nobleman, yet it disappeared, just in time for him to answer the enquiry of his butler 'Snipe, my Lord, or pheasant?' He instantly replied pheasant: thus completing his ninth dish of meat at that meal." I need not now tell you what is the state of his health.' This is a literal report of an anecdote told by the Speaker with much grave humor.

A few weeks afterwards: it was after his first levée, he said to me 'I know you remember a little trait or two I gave you of our friend's health on the Treasury bench, because I believe you have been pleased to mention what I said on that occasion. Now I will give you another bulletin. He did me the honor of attending my levée last night, which by the bye the leader of the Opposition did not do, & was graciously pleased to enquire after my health. "That" I said "was really of very little importance: but yours, my lord, is a national affair. I venture to hope you have not entirely disregarded my representations to you on that head, & that you take a little more care of yourself than heretofore." "Oh! I do indeed" he replied. "I very often take a cab at night & if you have both windows open, it is almost as good as walking home."' 'Almost as good!' exclaimed the valetudinarian Speaker with a rueful expression. 'A thorough draught & a north-east wind! And in a hack cab! What a combination for health!'

[74]

Dissolution of 1865. July.

The state of Lord Palmerston's health is really this. The gout, from which he never suffered much, is a pretence. The real complaint is an irritation in the bladder. Probably, there is nothing in itself fatal or dangerous, but its consequences are serious at his time of life in this respect; he is obliged to give up riding; his favorite & principal exercise; & the complaint breaks his faculty of sleep, which was his forté, & carried him through everything. Dr. Ferguson just before he died (this spring), said that six months must elapse before he could decide, whether Lord Palmerston could recover from this complaint, but Dr Ferguson, though a very clever man, was always an alarmist. His reign was the reign of terror.

[75]

1865

31st Augt. MaryAnne & I went to Raby & stayed a week. I believe it was the first reception of the Harry Vanes', since their accession. Raby a real castle—& vast: & though occasionally altered & 'improved', not substantially changed in character. The general effect feudal & Plantagenet. Though the country in the vicinity not beautiful, the immediate domain well wooded: a herd of 400 deer, & red deer also: but they never blend physically & socially; they live apart.

The Duchess a brilliant woman; sister of Lord Stanhope: she has the quickest, & the finest, perception of humor I know, with extraordinary power of expression; & the Stanhope wit; her conversation unceasing, but never long or wearying: a wondrous flow of drollery, information, social tattle, taste, eloquence: such a ceaseless flow of contemporary anecdote I never heard. And yet she never repeats.

The Duke makes a very good Duke: tall & dignified, but very natural, & though not exactly good-looking, a good presence & a good expression of countenance, kind eyes.

Affectionate to his step-children. Hers by her former marriage with Lord Dalmeny, eldest son of Earl of Rosebery. The grandfather yet living.

Her eldest son, Dalmeny, seemed to me very intelligent & formed for his time of life (not yet of age) & not a prig, which might be feared.

His younger brother, Everard Primrose, 17, very promising. Two sisters: one handsome, & both pleasing.

Then we went from the ancient to a modern Castle, Lowther: a splendid domain: parks & deer, mountains & lakes. The house convenient, & handsome in the interior, but the exterior deplorable, as might be expected from the Gothic of 1800 & Sir Smirke.

As my Lord receives no ladies, but would receive my wife, a female cousin, Lowther, & her brother, were present, & the rest a silent, but not scanty, court of retainers.

Then we returned to the South, to Ashridge Castle, Lord Brownlow's; also a modern erection by Wyatt, but gorgeous, & in a vast park of wonderfully sylvan beauty.

Lord Brownlow, a good deal beyond six feet high, slender, rather bent, with one lung already lost, & obliged to pass the winters at Madeira, intellectual, highly educated, with a complete sense of duty, & of soft & amiable disposition: living, as it were, on sufferance, but struggling to perform his great part. A devoted mother watches every glance & every wind; shares his annual exile, where she actually has not a single companion.

Brownlow's upper part of the face, the brow, the eyes, very fine; his fatal deficiency, the absence almost of chin: the distinctive mark of man, for animals have no chin: so he was thought always ill-looking—but since beards have become the fashion & he has become old enough to grow one, & that a famous one, he has turned out quite handsome. As Bernal Osborne said of a once-ill-looking fellow who became passable by being very hirsute, 'He has planted out his face.'

Adalbert Cust, B's only brother, has both his lungs, is as tall, well-formed & one of the handsomest young fellows in England. The day he came of age, his brother presented him with the title deeds of an estate of 6000£ per annum in the north of England. Winston (I think) near Raby: I went to see it with Duchess of Cleveland. The brothers were always devotedly attached to each other—naturally affectionate, their mother has studiously developed their mutual love.

Lady Marian a woman of commanding ability. Above the common height, a fine figure, but a countenance of animation & intelligence marred by a red & rough complexion. She always reminded me of Lady Blessington in face, when Lady B's beauty had departed: the eyes were the same, extremely sparkling. Lady Marian had also, like Lady Blessington, very pretty hands, which tell particularly in a large woman; well-shaped, & small, & plump, & white.

From Ashbridge we went to Woburn Abbey, & paid a visit of several days to Hastings Russell & his wife Lady Elizabeth, sister of Lady Salisbury. The present Duke of Bedford lives in perfect solitude, & fancies himself unable to encounter the world. I am told his abilities are good. He believes that his health is very bad: some say this is entirely imagination. Lord Carington, who knew him when he was a youth, told me, that he always hated his position, & shrunk with horror from its representation & responsibility. He detests the country, & country life: especially the provincial magnificence of grand seigneurs. 'Let me live always among chimney pots' he says.

When he was of age, he was returned to the House of Commons, & I remember him there for a session: he soon retired. A handsome man: with regular features & fine complexion, something of the beauty of the Stanhopes (his mother was daughter of Lord Harrington) & thin gold spectacles.

He must be now nearer sixty than fifty; nor is it probable, he will ever marry. He has two mistresses: one is his nurse; the other he visits daily & dines with her. She is not faithful to him: that's not wonderful, perhaps not necessary. The only person in society he ever sees except Hastings Russell is Poodle Byng, who recommended him to marry & get heirs. 'Why should I' said the Duke. 'Could I have a better son than Hastings?'

Hastings is his cousin, & will be, in all probability, the future

Duke: a young man, at least he looks young, though he has been married twenty years—good-looking, graceful, though hardly the middle size, very intelligent, well informed & well-meaning. The Duke gave him Oakley & £6000 a year, & expressed his wish also, that he would receive every year his friends at Woburn, which is kept up exactly as if His Grace resided there. Hastings has the entire management of the property: it is a principality. He prepares his budget every year like a Chancellor of the Exchequer: all the expenditure estimated in detail, the proposed improvements, alterations, repairs; farm-buildings, churches, schools, cottages. The Duke goes through every item in his solitary London house with scrutiny, & intention. The Duke builds cottages which cost 240 or 250£ a piece to which 30 per cent as Mr Bright says ought to be added for the expense of the plant in Woburn Park where all the materials for all the operations of the estate are prepared, & which is an establishment as large as the hugest factories & workshops in the North. Hastings objects to these costly cottages which are let to peasants receiving at the most 10/ per week at rents of 1/ or 1/6 per week, so that they are to live with all these conveniences, even luxuries, with incomes necessarily inadequate to their dwellings & the tastes which they produce.

Hastings showed some of them to Sir Edward Kerrison, a thorough country-gentleman, experienced in rural life. Kerrison was indignant. 'These are not cottages' he said 'these are villas.'

Woburn is fine from its greatness & completeness: everything that the chief seat of a princely English family requires. The house though not beautiful in its exterior is vast: the great quadrangle when lit up at night with its numerous & flashing windows reminded Bright, he said when on a visit there, of a factory. Then there are stables not unworthy of Chantilly, a riding house, a gallery of sculpture, the finest private one perhaps in the world. A mass of choice & rare collections of all kinds which have ᴜᴇᴇn accumulating for centuries: splendid books, rare MSS., some fine, many interesting pictures. A park of 3000 acres, with great variety, & undulation & wild scenes you would not expect in Bedfordshire: splendid oaks, unrivalled cedars; ornate gardens & wilderness drives.

And all this only 40 miles from town!

The Salisburys, our dear friends, & the Caringtons were there,

& Comte Pahlen, who gives the results of a life experienced in society with taste & terseness, & Odo Russell just arrived from Rome (where he is our Minister) via Paris.

He brought the new toy; Pharaoh's serpent. Quite a miracle! A most agreeable party, which it could not fail to be with such guests, & such a host & hostess, for Lady Elizabeth is quite worthy of her husband.

The predominant feature & organic deficiency of the Russell family is shyness. Even Hastings is not free from it, though he struggles to cover it with an air of uneasy gaiety.

[76]

1865

Lady Marian Alford (Ashridge) said 'Posterity remembers only one work of an author, but what that work shall be, Posterity can alone decide.'

1865

Some incomes of our Nobility—authentic.

The Duke of Northumberland recently deceased had more than 150,000 per annum.

The present Duke of Cleveland (Harry Vane) has £120,000 per annum aggregating in himself three fortunes: 80,000 per annum the Cleveland Duchy, enjoyed by his elder brother, who died less than two years ago: the Powlett fortune enjoyed by his second brother, Lord Wm. Powlett (Duke William of less than a year) & his own considerable appanage, which was nearly half a million & which he had increased, previous to his accession, by economy.

Lord Derby has £110,000 per annum.

Lord Lonsdale has about 60,000 per annum.*

Lord Brownlow has 90,000 per annum.

  all these incomes clear.

The late Lord Beauchamp left Elmley, after very amply providing for the junior members of the family, £45,000 per annum, clear. This family had a great talent for amassing. 'It will soon be

* Written below: 'Note 1872. Lord L. died & left exactly double this.'

£50,000 per annum' Lord St Germans, who was Elmley's uncle, said, when it was first mentioned, & who knew the Lygons well. I have heard that the late Lord left Elmley £100,000 Bank Stock, worth more than a quarter million sterling. Elmley was very proud of his personal property. Landed property was all show, he used to say.

The present Duke of Bedford's income is £220,000 per annum & he allows £40,000 per annum for repairs & agency. Duke of Cleveland told me this, & said, that he knew it as [a] matter of business. Hastings Russell told me, that from his experience of the management of great estates (& he managed this), taking tithes into consideration, which he did, he did not think that more than 50 per cent came net to the Proprietor.

Duke of Cleveland said that 'notwithstanding all the stories about, he thought Palmerston's affairs must be pretty well. He got nothing from Broadlands: that only kept itself up; but he had other property in Ireland & Yorkshire; though to be sure they might be mortgaged. Then there was Lady Palmerston's considerable fortune: a life interest in Lord Melbourne's estate not less than £12,000 per annum & her Cowper jointure at least 3000 per annum & he always in office—& no children. Yet there always had been these odd stories. But why he (Duke of C.) thought he must be well off now was this. 'Palmerston' he said 'had been always a great speculator', & some years ago he got hold of some slate quarries in Wales, & worked them with a couple of friends, one of whom was the Duke's brother William (William Powlett, late Duke of Cleveland). Now he had to settle his brother's affairs on his decease; & he found to his astonishment that his brother was getting 5000£ per annum at least for his share in these quarries, & his share was a very small one compared with that of Lord Palmerston.

2nd Duke of Wellington used to say with regard to Palmerston's embarrassed affairs 'The explanation is Hush Money.'

[77]

October 1865
Lord Palmerston's last joke

Lord Granville (Lord President) had a dairy farm near London: 100 cows, & they all died from the pestilence, now raging. And early in Octr., Lord Granville suddenly married, a very young lady indeed, 'sweet seventeen', he himself being upwards of 50 (though very young looking, & quite adapted to captivate the youngest). When told, Palmerston said 'So, having lost his cows, Granville has taken a heifer.'

Lord Palmerston died on the 18th Octr.

His decease was quite unexpected by Lady Palmerston, who thought it possible, that he might not be able to bear the late hours of the House of Commons another Session but was resolved he should meet the new House of Commons in 1866 as their leader, because as the majority was returned as a demonstration of confidence in him, he was bound not to retire. If, however, the late hours were found too great a trial, Lord Palmerston was to go to the House of Lords, remaining Premier. And Lady Palmerston thought, that this arrangement might go on for years.

This may be quite relied on.

A PPENDIX

'rather to tune your mind, than to guide your pen'

Benjamin Disraeli revealed the public image he wanted his biographers to create in this letter of 27 March 1860 to Francis Espinasse.[1] Apparently, he had objected to a sketch of his life which had already been published; for a few weeks earlier Espinasse had written to him: 'I have received from Mr. Mackenzie of Glasgow, the proprietor & publisher of the "Imperial Dictionary of Universal Biography", a communication respecting a memoir of yourself contributed by me to that work.' Espinasse informed Disraeli that he regretted the inaccuracies in his account, which had been based on various sources, including an obituary of Isaac D'Israeli in the *Gentleman's Magazine*. He wished to correct these mistakes, such as 'the fable of your connection with the "Representative",' the disastrous newspaper venture of his youth which Disraeli was anxious for the world to forget. 'Accuracy being so desirable, I shall be extremely happy to re-write the memoir from any data which you may be kind enough to furnish,' Espinasse promised.[2]

Disraeli replied with the letter of 27 March, though certainly no biographer striving for accuracy could have relied upon the 'autobiographical memoranda' it contained.

Confidential

Grosvenor Gate. Mar. 27. 60

Dear Sir,

As I understand, that the Memoir of my father, in the 'Univ. Biog^y', is to precede mine, it will be unnecessary for me to touch upon some points I must otherwise have noticed. Nor, indeed, in

---

[1] Hughenden Papers A/X/B/1. (A short addendum on an article by George Smythe is omitted.)

[2] 4 March 1860: ibid./2.

this confidential memorandum is there, probably, anything, that will be of absolute use to you as regards myself, but it may prevent the repetition of mis[s]tatements, wh. have, perhaps, been too long permitted to pass unnoticed.

I was born Dec. 21, 1805 & my education was strictly private, wh. is perhaps all that need be said. I was at school for two or three years under the Revd. Dr Cogan, a Greek scholar of eminence, who had contributed notes to the A[e]schylus of Bishop Blomfield, & was himself the Editor of the Greek Gnomic Poets. After this, I was with a private tutor for two years in my own County, & my education was severely classical. Too much so: in the pride of boyish erudition, I edited the Idonesian Eclogue of Theocritus wh. was privately printed. This was my first production: puerile pedantry.

My father, who always lived in seclusion, & during the last thirty years of his life almost uninterruptedly in Bucks, had one powerful friend, who offered to provide for me in one of the offices of the Court of Chancery. It was a post, wh., in routine, would have given me, in due course, a better income than any other public office, &, if pursued with diligence & ability, led to some of the highest prizes in the profession. To be admitted as a Solicitor was a necessary qualification, & an intimate friend of my father assisted me in this respect—but altho' my life was, & wd. have been, little more than a form, I soon relinquished it, from a restlessness wh. then influenced me, & rendered travel absolutely necessary. In due course, my brother was offered the same opportunity, & the pursuit being one adapted to his character, he has, at a comparatively early period of life, risen to the post of Registrar of the Court of Chancery, one of dignity & great emolument.

Both my brothers were at Winchester, for wh. I was intended. This is the reason of my being often described as an alumnus of that public school.

When I was quite a youth, I made the acquaintance of the late Mr. Lockhart, & hung about him, as boys do about the first distinguished man with whom they become acquainted. In the year 1825, Mr. Lockhart, who then lived in Scotland, undertook, with the countenance of Mr Canning, to edit the Representative newspaper. In making his preliminary arrangements, he often made use of me, & I was delighted with his confidence. Sometime after, when in Italy, I took up an English magazine, & found 'a son of Mr Disraeli' described as the Editor of that paper, wh. had been a failure. I never was Editor of the paper; I never wrote a line in the paper; I was never asked to write a line in the paper. At the time of its appearance, I did not know I cd. write. But the mythus was established, & effected its object, it shielded Mr Lockhart, who was an expert in all the nebulous chicanery of these literary intrigues. Unfortunately, in this case, the man of straw he had fixed on, became eminent, & a newspaper failure, of nearly forty years ago, is remembered from its being the subject of a literary forgery.

Being upon this subject, I may venture to observe, that I do not suppose that any man of literary habits, who has so long been connected with public life, ever wrote less in the newspapers than myself. But I have never contradicted any assertion to the contrary; & for an obvious reason. I shd. have hurt the feelings of every journalist in the country.

With respect to the statement in the 'Gentleman's Mag^e' respecting my father & Mr. Murray, & of wh. I was unaware, it is hardly necessary to enter into the reasons why, nearly forty years ago, my father withdrew his confidence from Mr Murray. The incident could have had no reference to any relations between myself & Mr Murray, for that gentleman subsequently published several works for me, among them 'Contarini Fleming' (1831).

Vivian Grey was published 26–7 anonymously.
Young Duke   ”   29.

In that year, I left England, for the second time, in order to travel more extensively than hitherto. I was absent until the end of 1831 & shd. not have returned but as a Candidate for the Boro' of High Wycomb[e], in the immediate neighbourhood of my father's residence, against the Hon. Chas Grey, the son of the Prime Minister.

I was brought forward by the old Corporation, & proposed by the Tory Mayor, John Carter Esq. The Tories were influential men, but a very small minority. I made a coalition bet^n them & the Radicals, whose leader obtained the famous letters of Hume & O'Connell, neither of whom I had ever seen; & wh. led to the other mythus of my being sent down to Wycomb[e] by those gentlemen.

I never stood for Mary[le]bone, tho' I was asked immediately after the loss of the Wycomb[e] Election, & issued an address.

I may mention, that the contest bet[n] myself & Colonel Grey was a neck & neck race; & it was repeated in 1835 when I stood for the Boro' at the request of Sir Robert Peel, & was supported by precisely the same combination.

I ought to have mentioned, that I published in 1831-2 'C. Fleming' & 'Alroy'—both written while I was abroad—& the latter planned & partly composed at Jerusalem, wh. I believe I have mentioned in the preface of the later popular editions. In these days of rapid locomotion, my travels go for nothing—but I was in Syria, Asia Minor, & ascended the Nile to Nubia.

1836-7 'Henrietta Temple' & 'Venetia'.

Returned to Parliament for Maidstone *1837*. The Queen's first Parliament, & I have never been out of Parliament since.

Returned for Shrewsbury 1841 & sate for it six years.

1844-5-6 'Coningsby', 'Sybil', & 'Tancred' tho' the latter was not published until the spring of 1848—having been too much engaged in Parliament to finish it.

After the death of Ld. George Bentinck, was chosen Leader of the Tory party in the House of Commons; at the commencement of the Sess. 1849. Sir John Buller & Mr. Miles were deputed formally to announce to me the choice—& I had the satisfaction in due season, of recognising their undeviating fidelity to myself, by making one a Baronet, & elevating the other to the Peerage.

I found the Tory party, in the Ho. of Commons, when I acceded to its chief management, in a state of great depression & disorganisation. Lord George Bentinck had only numbered 120 in his motion on the Irish Railways, wh. was to try our strength in the new Parliament.

By a series of motions to relieve the Agricultural Interest by revising & partially removing the local taxation of the country, I withdrew the Tory party gradually from the hopeless question of Protection, rallied all those members who were connected either personally, or by their constituencies, with the land, & finally brought the state of parties in the House of Commons to nearly a tie.

This led, in 1851, to the offer of the Government of the Country to Ld. Derby, wh. he declined, but wh. he accepted in 1852.

I was then called to the Privy Council, appointed Chan[r] of the

Exchequer, & became Leader of the House of Commons without
ever having been in office, wh. I believe never happened before,
except in the case of Mr Pitt, when he was made Chan^r of the
Exchequer in Ld Shelburne's Government; & for as short a period.

In 1853 The University of Oxford conferred on me the degree
of D.C.L. with a demonstration of feeling, on the part of the
University, wh. has never been equalled, & is still remembered.

I ought to have observed, that, at the general election of 1847,
I was chosen Member for the County of Buckingham, witht. a
contest, & I have been returned five times for that County. This is
the event in my public life, wh. has given me the greatest satisfaction.

Lord George Bentinck was very firm to me, & in 1850 or 51,
I took the opportunity of recording his career in a work in which
I have attempted to treat contemporary politics with truth.

In Feby 1858, I was again appointed C of Ex^r & Leader of the
Ho. of Comm., & resigned June 1859.

I have answered your appeal witht. reserve. Perhaps, probably,
there is nothing in all this of wh. you can avail yourself. It is
rather to tune your mind, than to guide your pen. Details in contemporary biography can hardly be touched witht. great delicacy
& reserve. One shd. only record events, but it is desirable that
they shd. be true.

I have written this with haste, for your letter has reached me
at a moment of great pressure. I hope it is rather egotistical, than
vain; but at all events excuse it.

I shd. have said that in *1839* I married, & it is the complete
domestic happiness wh. I then achieved, wh. has mainly sustained
me in a career of considerable trial.

My wife, with whom I had been long acquainted, was the
widow of my colleague at Maidstone Mr. Wyndham Lewis, &
was herself the daughter of Captain Viney Evans R. N. son of
General Sir James Viney by a sister of the late William Scrope
Esq., of Castle Combe, Wilts with whose distinguished works
you are well acquainted, & who represented in his person the
most ancient family of noble blood in England.

Have the kindness to acknowledge the receipt of this packet &
believe me,

faithfully yours

Francis Espinasse Esq   D.

Prime Ministers from Peel to Palmerston and Some Members of Their Cabinets[1]

1834–35

Sir R. Peel, P.M. & Chr. of Exchr.
Lord Lyndhurst, Ld. Chr.
J. C. Herries, Secy. at War
Duke of Wellington, For. Secy.
H. Goulburn, Home Secy.
Lord Ellenborough, Pres. Bd. of Con.
Lord Aberdeen, Secy. War & Cols.

1835–41

Lord Melbourne, P.M.
Lord J. Russell, Home Secy.
Lord Palmerston, For. Secy.
Lord Lansdowne, Ld. Pres. of Coun.
(T. B. Macaulay, Secy. at War)

1841–46

Peel, P.M.
Lyndhurst, Ld. Chr.
Goulburn, Chr. of Exchr.
Lord Stanley, Secy. War & Cols.
Duke of Buckingham, Ld. Py. Seal
Ellenborough, Pres. Bd. of Con.
Aberdeen, For. Secy.
Wellington, witht. office

[1] The offices named are those held at the formation of the Cabinet; parentheses indicate ministers who joined later.

149

Sir J. Graham, Home Secy.
(W. E. Gladstone, Pres. Bd. of Tr.)
(S. Herbert, Secy. at War)

1846–52
Russell, P.M.
Palmerston, For. Secy.
Macaulay, Paymaster-Gen.

1852
Derby, P.M.
B. Disraeli, Chr. of Exchr.
Lord Malmesbury, For. Secy.
Lord Salisbury, Ld. Py. Seal
Sir J. Pakington, Secy. War & Cols.
Lord J. Manners, F. Comm. of Works
Duke of Northumberland, F. Ld. Admy.
Herries, Pres. Bd. of Con.
J. W. Henley, Pres. Bd. of Tr.

1852–55
Aberdeen, P.M.
Gladstone, Chr. of Exchr.
Palmerston, Home Secy.
Russell, For. Secy.
Graham, F. Ld. Admy.
Herbert, Secy. at War
Lansdowne, witht. office

1855–58
Palmerston, P.M.
Gladstone, Chr. of Exchr.
Graham, F. Ld. Admy.
Herbert, Secy. for Cols.
Lansdowne, witht. office
(Sir G. C. Lewis, Chr. of Exchr.)
(Russell, Secy. for Cols.)

1858–59

Derby, P.M.
Disraeli, Chr. of Exchr.
Malmesbury, For. Secy.
Salisbury, Ld. Pres. of Coun.
Pakington, F. Ld. Admy.
Manners, F. Comm. of Works
Henley, Pres. Bd. of Tr.
Lord Stanley, Secy. for Cols.
Gen. J. Peel, Secy. for War
Ellenborough, Pres. Bd. of Con.
(Sir E. Bulwer-Lytton, Secy. for Cols.)

1859–65

Palmerston, P.M.
Gladstone, Chr. of Exchr.
Herbert, Secy. for War
Lewis, Home Secy.
Russell, For. Secy.
(C. P. Villiers, Pres. Poor Law Bd.)
(Lord de Grey, Secy. for War)

Key to Section Numbers in Original Manuscript

Reminiscences—Ms.		Reminiscences—Ms.	
1.	1	30.	26
2.	69	31.	17
3.	2	32.	35
4.	3	33.	39
5.	40	34.	38
6.	27	35.	36
7.	5	36.	15
8.	4	37.	37
9.	30	38.	49
10.	11	39.	50
11.	14	40.	51
12.	42	41.	63
13.	9	42.	8
14.	10	43.	71
15.	12	44.	43
16.	16	45.	41
17.	20	46.	45
18.	7	47.	46
19.	13	48.	47
20.	28	49.	54
21.	21	50.	29
22.	22	51.	19
23.	23	52.	70
24.	24	53.	62
25.	25	54.	31
26.	18	55.	44
27.	32	56.	6
28.	33	57.	52
29.	34	58.	53

Reminiscences—Ms.		Reminiscences—Ms.	
59.	56	69.	66
60.	59	70.	67
61.	48	71.	68
62.	55	72.	77
63.	58	73.	73
64.	60	74.	74
65.	57	75.	75
66.	61	76.	76
67.	64	77.	72
68.	65		

BIBLIOGRAPHY

This brief bibliography for the general reader must omit many more titles than it can include, and it naturally suffers from the idiosyncratic choices of its compilers. The most complete biography of Disraeli is by W. F. Monypenny and G. E. Buckle, *The Life of Benjamin Disraeli, Earl of Beaconsfield* (London: John Murray, 6 vols., 1910–20). Modern readers will probably prefer a one-volume version by Robert Blake, *Disraeli* (London: Eyre & Spottiswoode, 1966), which has a good bibliography and a list of Disraeli's works. Disraeli has, understandably, been better served as a politician than a novelist. Muriel Masefield, *Peacocks and Primroses: A Survey of Disraeli's Novels* (London: Geoffrey Bles, 1953) is useful for what the second half of its title promises. A short critical study of the novels, with bibliography, is by Richard Levine, *Benjamin Disraeli* (New York: Twayne Publishers, Inc., 1968).

Two general texts which put the first two-thirds of the nineteenth century into historical perspective are by E. L. Woodward, *The Age of Reform, 1815–1870* (Oxford: Clarendon Press, 2nd edn., 1962), and Asa Briggs, *The Age of Improvement* (London: Longmans, Green and Co., 1959). G. Kitson Clark, *The Making of Victorian England* (New York: Atheneum, 1962, 1967 edn.) and G. M. Young, *Victorian England: Portrait of an Age* (London: Oxford University Press, 2nd edn., 1953, 1966 edn.) are stimulating interpretative narratives.

It is possible to cite only a few specialized books on the many topics mentioned in the *Reminiscences*. Ellen Moers, *The Dandy: Brummell to Beerbohm* (New York: Viking Press, 1960) and E. Beresford Chancellor, *Life in Regency and Early Victorian Times: An Account of the Days of Brummell and D'Orsay, 1800 to 1850* (London: B. T. Batsford, Ltd., [c. 1927]) depict, with illustrations, the social milieu of Disraeli's days as a dandy. John Timbs, *Clubs and Club Life in London* (London: J. C. Hotten [1873]) is a handy anecdotal guide to that most important aspect of a gentleman's existence in the nineteenth century. Ralph Nevill, ed., *Leaves from the Note-Books of Lady Dorothy Nevill* (London: Macmillan and Co., Ltd., 1907) and T. H. S. Escott, *Society in the Country House* (Philadelphia: G. W. Jacobs & Co., [c. 1906]) are two samples of the contemporary or nearly contemporary sources on the upper-class world in which Disraeli eventually moved. A weightier chronicle, also deeply concerned with politics, is *The Greville Memoirs*, the most complete edition of which is by Lytton Strachey and Roger Fulford (London: Macmillan & Co., 8 vols., 1938).

More specifically, Norman Gash, *Politics in the Age of Peel* (New York: W. W. Norton & Co., Inc., 1953, 1971 edn.) is an excellent study; and J. B. Conacher, *The Peelites and the Party System, 1846–52* (Newton Abbot: David & Charles, 1972) is a short account of a particularly important parliamentary group. Two books on foreign policy are R. W. Seton-Watson, *Britain and Europe 1789–1914* (Cambridge: Cambridge University Press, 1937, 1945 edn.) and Kenneth Bourne, *The Foreign Policy of Victorian England, 1830–1902* (Oxford: Clarendon Press, 1970). Gordon Wright, *France in Modern Times, 1760 to the Present* (Chicago: Rand McNally & Co., 1960, 1970 edn.) provides in its second part a good introduction to the period 1815–70. Walter E. Houghton, *The Victorian Frame of Mind, 1830–1870* (New Haven: Yale University Press, 1957, 1963 edn.) uses contemporary literature extensively to analyse the emotional, intellectual, and moral attitudes of the age. Kathleen Tillotson, *Novels of the Eighteen-Forties* (Oxford: Clarendon Press, 1954) helps to place Disraeli's Young England trilogy in the literary perspective of its decade. A glimpse of the world of science is caught in *The Autobiography of Charles Darwin and Selected Letters* (New York: Dover Publications Inc., 1892, 1958 edn.), Francis Darwin, ed.

The subjects of the books in the following list are some of the more prominent figures in the *Reminiscences*:

Brightfield, Myron F., *John Wilson Croker* (Berkeley: University of California Press, 1940)

Gash, Norman, *Sir Robert Peel* (Totowa, N. J.: Rowman and Littlefield, 1972)

Guest, Ivor, *Napoleon III in England* (London: British Technical & General Press, 1952)

Jones, W. D., *Lord Derby and Victorian Conservatism* (Oxford: Basil Blackwell, 1956)

Longford, Elizabeth, *Victoria R.I.* (London: Pan Books, Ltd., 1964, 1966 edn.); and *Wellington: Pillar of State* (New York: Harper & Row, Publishers; London: Weidenfeld & Nicolson, 1972)

Magnus, Philip, *Gladstone: A Biography* (New York: E. P. Dutton & Co., Inc., 1954, 1964 edn.; London: John Murray, 1954)

Malmesbury, Earl of, *Memoirs of an Ex-Minister* (London: Longmans, Green, and Co., new edn., 1885)

Martin, Theodore, *A Life of Lord Lyndhurst* (London: John Murray, 1883)

Pope-Hennessy, James, *Monckton Milnes* (New York: Farrar, Straus & Cudahy, Inc., 2 vols., 1955 edn.; London: Constable)

Prest, John, *Lord John Russell* (London: Macmillan, 1972)

Ridley, Jasper, *Lord Palmerston* (London: Panther Books, 1970, 1972 edn.)

Sadleir, Michael, *Blessington-D'Orsay, A Masquerade* (London: Constable & Co Ltd, 1933); and *Bulwer: A Panorama* (Boston: Little, Brown, and Company, 1931; London: Constable & Co., 1931).

INDEX

An * indicates that the name appears in the list of prime ministers and some members of their cabinets, pages 149–51.